GURLESQUE

the new grrly, grotesque, burlesque poetics

GURLESQUE

the new grrly, grotesque, burlesque poetics

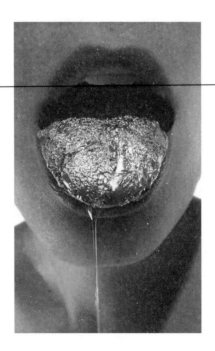

saturnalia books

Saturnalia Books
105 Woodside Rd.
Ardmore, PA 19003
info@saturnaliabooks.com

ISBN: 978-0-9818591-4-9
Library of Congress Control Number: 2009933612

Book Design by Saturnalia Books
Printing by McNaughton & Gunn

Cover Art: Hard Wear (Tongue Gliding)
© Lauren Kalman
Digital print, laminated on acrylic, 2006

Distributed by:
University Press of New England
1 Court Street
Lebanon, NH 03766
800-421-1561

Acknowledgments

This project has been an utter pleasure for its two editors. First and foremost, we'd like to thank our poet-contributors, whose work inspires, astounds and throws us, for letting us include them in this anthology. We like to say that we consider each of these women a bad-ass, in the best possible sense, and have never taken it for granted that they would be so utterly agreeable, generous, and supportive of this project. Our gratitude, too, to their presses for letting us reprint their work here.

We likewise thank the visual artists whose work is featured in these pages, for allowing us to extend this conversation and theory beyond the genre of poetry, ~~and for granting us permission to publish these reproductions of their work.~~ Thanks to their galleries and agents as well for their generosity.

We would also like to thank Henry Israeli at Saturnalia Books for being an enthusiastic editor for this project, and having the vision and commitment to bring it to print. Johannes Göransson and Danielle Pafunda have provided valuable editorial suggestions and support, as have Jed Rasula, Susan Rosenbaum, and Ed Pavlic. Matthea Harvey and Ariana Reines, in addition to being wonderful contributors of their own work, brought several exciting visual artists to our attention. And we thank Zach Kolodjeski, a student worker at Columbia College Chicago, who made our lives easier through his assistance, and the English departments at Columbia College and LSU for their support.

Finally, we thank our families: our husbands, Josef Horacek and Rob Morris, for their valued opinions and their crucial ability to be the fully and deeply egalitarian partners that they are; and our children, Sasha and Sebastian Glenum-Horacek and Willa and Jem Bywater, for demanding and providing love, wonder, and the impetus for radical change in the world.

—Lara Glenum and Arielle Greenberg

Other books by Lara Glenum

The Hounds of No
Maximum Gaga

Other books by Arielle Greenberg

My Kafka Century
Given
Starting Today: 100 Poems for Obama's First 100 Days
(as editor with Rachel Zucker)
Women Poets on Mentorship: Efforts & Affections
(as editor with Rachel Zucker)

TABLE OF CONTENTS

*

SOME NOTES ON THE ORIGIN OF THE (TERM) GURLESQUE

The Gurlesque was born between about 1960 and 1982 (it was a long labor) (these are the years generally considered, by the way, the birth of Generation X) in Burma and Ohio and Korea and New York and Olympia, WA and other places. Her ancestor was Ophelia, running around singing spooky songs with her hair all drippy. Her grandmother was Alice in Wonderland and Eloise and Ramona the Pest. Her mom was a Second Wave feminist and a hippie and a lady who had never been to a consciousness-raising group but sometimes watched *Maude* and an immigrant and a farmwife and a former Girl Scout. Her mom was Anne Waldman and Anne Rice and Sylvia Plath and Barbara Guest and V.C. Andrews and Angela Carter. She had aunts, too, like Hannah Weiner and Kathy Acker and Katharine Dunn and Amy Gerstler and Annie Sprinkle. Her aunts were Angela Davis and Nan Goldin and Hello Kitty and the Guerilla Girls and Dolly Parton and Exene Cervenka and Cindy Sherman and Poly Styrene, the fifteen-year-old multiracial girl with braces on her teeth screaming "*Some* people say little girls should be seen and not heard, but I say: *Oh, bondage, up yours!*" as she fronted the band the X-Ray Spex in a 1977 punk club in London. She was a pink and black and yellow and red and brown and rainbow-colored silver baby, and she was a girl baby except when she was a boy baby, which was sometimes.

*

The Gurlesque was born of black organza witch costumes and the silver worn-out sequins mashed between scratchy pink tutu netting and velvet unicorn paintings and arena rock ballads and rainbow iron-on glitter decals and self-mutilation and anorexia and bulimia and fighting back and Renaissance Faires and teen sex and zines and cutting and *Sassy* and joy and ecstasy and abortion and the Pill and road kill and punk shows and panties and incest and ice cream and rape and we mean this very seriously. No means no, asshole. And yes means yes. And girl means girl except when it doesn't, which is sometimes.

*

The Gurlesque was born of a three-stamen'ed hydra flower.

*

I decided on the term *Gurlesque* because of the way it sounds like it comes from
the stuff that the Gurlesque comes from: 1. The Carnivalesque. 2. The Burlesque
(and the Neo-Burlesque). 3. The Riot Grrls. I'll come back to this.

Also, the Grotesque.

*

The very first thing I ever wrote about the Gurlesque, a term I coined, was a
review of Chelsey Minnis' *Zirconia* published in issue three of the online
Electronic Poetry Review, in which I said: "[This style is]...not...limited to this
work or this author, because the particular brand of sensuality / sentimentality at
work here is one which I believe is in the zeitgeist: a 'gurlesque' aesthetic, a femi-
nine, feminist incorporating of the grotesque and cruel with the spangled and
dreamy."

*

Hey, Lara, are you "performing the Gurlesque" over there in your essay? Do
you want to go to lunch later or look at some terrifying art or lactate together?
What are you wearing? Can you please explain the carnivalesque now? What
about the history of the burlesque? The grotesque of the female body and
Kristeva's ideas about the body as a site of horror? Ok, great, thanks so much,
you're a peach.

*

Look, the Gurlesque is just something I saw. (I see dead people.—*The Sixth*

Sense) (I see words.—Hannah Weiner) It's not a movement or a camp or a clique. Most of these women don't even know each other, never went to school together. They'd rather not belong to a club that would blah blah blah. Frankly, Lara and I were surprised any of these bad-asses would agree to be in this book.

(And I should say, not even these poets do the Gurlesque watusi all of the time. For some of these writers, the Gurlesque is just a tendency that occasionally crops up. Some did it more in their early stuff. Some are doing it more later. Some only do it now and then. Some are 24/7 Gurlesque rockers. Being in this anthology doesn't mean anything about the poets in particular: we are just trotting these poems out on our sideshow stage because of what we see in them. Because we love them.)

Anyway, I just saw this thing happening, starting to happen, and because God gave names to all the animals, I named it. It was 2001. I was in graduate school in a city almost completely sunk in snow and poverty and sadness and rape culture (see Alice Sebold's memoir), and I was trying to ward off the agoraphobia and anxiety attacks by reading books of poetry by young women. It was 2001: there were suddenly a lot of books and journals of poetry by young women. *Fence*, founded by Rebecca Wolff, had made a super-big splash. A couple cities over, Juliana Spahr and Jena Osman and others had just lit some fires in Buffalo and were now out in the world, making *Chain*. A *Chain*-linked *Fence*, and *Tinfish* edited by Susan Schultz, and a woman running St. Mark's Poetry Project, and the wom-po listserv: it was super-exciting. There were these wild books of poetry by young women coming out in America; there were wild new presses begun by young women in America.

Can I call what I saw *similarities*? I could, but I'd rather call them ghosts: time-ghosts rising up from the pages of these young books. Brenda Shaughnessy's first book (*Interior with Sudden Joy*, FSG 2000). Chelsey Minnis' first book (*Zirconia*, Fence Books, 2001). Brenda Coultas' early chapbooks. Catherine Wagner's first book (*Miss America*, Fence Books, 2001). Others.

*

So I was reading all these books where women were writing about and through femininity in what seemed to me an exciting and new way: brashly, playfully, provocatively, indulgently, and while these were overtly poems of women's experiences, of the female body and of sexuality, poems rooted, you could argue, in the understanding of America as a rape culture, there appeared almost no trace of the earnestness, sensitivity or self-seriousness that marked many such poems stemming from Second Wave feminism. In the place of a high-minded or moral stance, these new poems had people bashing one another with candelabras in them, they had unicorns in them, and sequins, and swear words, and vomit. In place of confessional narrative there was fragment and disjuncture, prose and chant. These poems were silly and scary, pretty and dirty, wild and demanding. Wow, I thought, this is a kind of women's poetry I can really get behind! I feel like I know this poetry.

I knew where it was coming from, because I had the same ghosts, the same gut. Same mix tapes. Different lipstick shades. Same riot grrl zines. Different families of origin. But yeah. It was happening. Something. (*It's all happening!*—the teenage girl groupies in *Almost Famous*.)

So I coined a term—the Gurlesque, mashing together sounds and consonants and ideas from the Bakhtin carnivalesque theory of upside-down spectacle-land public-art subversion and the glitter pasties and sneer and drag and pratfalls of the burlesque performer and the "take back the girl, fuck up the spelling" riot grrl punk rock music zine activism movement.

And I wrote about the term in a couple of book reviews I published and then talked about it at Small Press Traffic in San Francisco at the behest of the rad Elizabeth Treadwell who was director and doing a series on new movements in poetry in 2002, and that talk was put online, and somehow people found it. And other people found the term and used it in their book reviews and dissertations. And I was also seeing the Gurlesque happening in visual art by young women and music by young women and this was so exciting to me but I had a full-time teaching job and a baby on the way and I didn't have time to write about all of it. And eventually Lara and I met when Action Books put out our dark, spooky, womanly, loud books at the same time and we toured around the South together with our baby girls born days apart, reading poems about the uterus and genocide and earrings and holes and pearls, and eventually Lara asked if I wanted to edit a collection of Gurlesque poems with her, and I said, *right on, sister.*

*

On Riot Grrl:

It can be argued that riot grrl was no more a movement than the Gurlesque is— maybe it, too, was more a *moment*, an aesthetic, an attitude erupting from the socio-political-historical-artistic zeitgeist. Back in the early '90s, at the same time that "Take Back the Night" rallies against rape were happening on college campuses, Anita Hill was testifying against Clarence Thomas, and there were marches on Washington for choice, young women in the punk and indie rock scenes got tired of seeing only boys, boys, boys on the stage and the cover of the fanzines, got tired of being groped while crowd-surfing, got tired of all the male rock critics holding forth, got tired of the general testosterone levels in the scene at large. So girls started their own punk fanzines in which they could talk about their periods and eating disorders and sexism and craft projects (like "make your own zine bookshelf" or "make your own glittery guitar strap") along with concert and record reviews and shout-outs to friends. Girls started forming their own, girl-only mosh pits in the front of rock clubs. Girls held events. Girls started bands.

There was a look associated with riot grrl, which pulled elements from Sesame Street childhoods, Goth, punk, grunge, and ballet class, and it was a look that lots of young women interested in underground music and culture were wearing at that time: that look often involved thrift store Catholic schoolgirl skirts, rock t-shirts, '50s sequin cardigans, combat boots, old metal lunchboxes carried as purses, plastic kiddie barrettes in Manic Panic-dyed hair. Oh, and some grrls wrote words like "bitch" and "cunt" and "dyke" on themselves with black marker or lipstick. Riot grrls also wanted to take back language, take back girlhood, take back their lives.

The general mood of it was righteous indignation and humor and anger and shyness and confidence and insecurity and unity and non-conformity and in-fighting and prettiness and ugliness and performance and honesty and activism and DIY art making and transgression and revolution. Revolution girl-style *now*.

There were no leaders, though there were rock stars and zine editors who were the face of riot grrl. There were a few meetings held in major cities and some specific happenings, but mostly girls came together through the mail and at shows. As soon as the mainstream media got hold of it (*Newsweek* got there by 1992), the movement kind of fizzled out of fear of co-opting. No one wanted to be told who they were or what they looked like or what they did or did not stand for: that was the whole point. And another thing: this was not a mainstream movement! Who wants to be mainstream? And anyway, by 1996, the Spice Girls were pop sensations with a "girl power" slogan and it all felt very icky.

Perhaps the most important thing to say is that riot grrl—the music and zines, the attitude—opened up a space within the subculture of indiepunkunderground-whatever for young women to start skipping and running and veering toward a new kind of feminism, a new bunch of strategies to talk about misogyny and how to change the world. That's all. Riot grrls just changed the world.

*

Sometimes I only want to talk about the Gurlesque as the riot grrl I was in 1992, when I was publishing my zine: I want to be wearing a blue velvet cocktail '60s dress and ripped fishnets and cut-off combat boots and a ball-chain necklace with a glow-in-the-dark plastic skeleton hanging from it and ponytails and a nose ring; I want to be marching for choice with ACT-UP, chanting "we're here, we're queer, we're fabulous, get used to it"; I want to be making my own peanut butter and buying ninety-nine cent lipstick at the drugstore and working at a homeless shelter; I want to be trading for seven inch records and getting the last train back from the show.

Sometimes I only want to talk about the Gurlesque at a table covered with a velvet cloth where hovering just behind me are the White Witch Goddess, the godmother of the Gurlesque, Stevie Nicks, with her black tulle sleeve-points dripping down and her Victorian boots laced up, with her baby doll facial features and her cocaine nosebleeds.

Or I only want to talk about the Gurlesque accompanied by a performance by infamous underground comix girl Dame Darcy, whom I met in New York in the 90s, and Darcy would be dressed in thrift store moldy camisoles and petticoats, drunkenly playing her accordion over loops of morbid, old-timey looking hand-made films about vampire wolf lovers and PEZ-dispenser witch girlfriends.

*

What else is exciting and meaningful is how all of this stuff seems to be happening in activism and music and art made by young women at the *exact same time* as the poetry. Freaky! Not a coincidence! A time-ghost!

*

Or, the Gurlesque would be best theorized about while riding on the back of a vintage convertible at the ratty, muggy Mermaid Parade that's held at Coney Island every summer solstice, where girls and not-girls dressed in their mermaid finest and in various states of undress and full-body tattoos zoom around in the shadows of ill-repaired amusement park rides from the 1920s, watched by an array of New York City hipsters and gang bangers and families eating hot dogs and attending the performance-art freak-shows held nearby.

*

Um, do you think this Gurlesque stuff is just, like, already *over*? Or not really all that exciting or shocking or new or different? Sort of stupid? I could care less.

It's just something I see happening in the world. And Lara sees it, too. We see words. We see dead people. So there.

It's just words. It's just the apocalypse with girls riding in bareback on black horses. It's just the second coming of a baby girl messiah.

*

The thing is, girls are kind of used to being called stupid and late and boring and dumb. Bring on the sticks and stones.

And if you put this poetry down then you are fucking with the girly and this whole thing is about fucking with the girly so, hey, welcome to the party, but if you're a boy you have to stand at the back of the room while we girls get down at the front.

*

Clitoral (instead of seminal) to the Gurlesque is Playing with (Fucking with) the Girly.

*

And what is girly, anyway? Renaissance Faire wench? Daisy Dukes-Daisy Mae inbred bumpkin? Japanese fetish Goth Lolita street fashion? Marilyn Chambers Ivory Snow porn girl? Unicorn princess? Cheerleader? Stripper? Rock Star? Mermaid? Activist? Slut? Virgin? Queer? Fishnets? Knee socks? Lip-gloss? Lollipops?

Yes.

Take the girly. Shake it up. Make a milkshake. Make it throw up.

—Arielle Greenberg, 2009

THEORY OF THE GURLESQUE: BURLESQUE, GIRLY KITSCH, AND THE FEMALE GROTESQUE

If you have doubts about the value of an anthology, know that this particular one does not put itself forward as a monument or a hermetically sealed crypt. This anthology is intended as a portal, as the beginning of a conversation whose end remains unseen. The eighteen poets and nine visual artists included herein are not part of any unified movement; they are scattershot points on an unmarked graph. What we are attempting to do is trace out a few possible constellations.

The Gurlesque describes an emerging field of female artists now in their 20s, 30s, and early 40s who, taking a page form the burlesque, perform their femininity in a campy or overtly mocking way. Their work assaults the norms of acceptable female behavior by irreverently deploying gender stereotypes to subversive ends.

In what follows, I'd like to briefly outline some of the theoretical tangents germane to Gurlesque poetics: namely, burlesque and camp, "girly kitsch," and the female grotesque.

"Creatures of an alien sex": The Burlesque

Many people associate burlesque with its 1930s incarnation, the strip-tease, which was a far cry from the early years of the burlesque theater—the 1840s to the 1860s—which were pioneered almost exclusively by troupes of female actresses under the direction of other women in Victorian London. Their dance hall repertoire was an antecedent of vaudeville, only much more socially explosive. Scholar Robert C. Allen, in his seminal work on burlesque, *Horrible Prettiness*, surmises that burlesque "presented a world without limits, a world turned upside down and inside out in which nothing was above being brought down to earth. In that world, things that should be kept separate were united in grotesque hybrids. Meanings refused to stay put. Anything might happen."[i]

Emily Layne Fargo writes:

> Burlesque performers also literally usurped male power by taking on male roles onstage.... [H]owever, female burlesque performers were never trying to present a convincing, realistic portrayal of a man onstage. Instead, they were utilizing their masculine attire as a sort of fetish object, in fact emphasizing their feminine sexuality by contrasting it with markers of masculinity... These practices, of course, ultimately emphasized the constructed nature of both genders, calling into question accepted gender roles themselves.[ii]

The effect of such "unladylike" conduct led at least one critic to deem burlesque performers neither men nor women but "creatures of an alien sex, parodying both."[iii] And parody, as Baudrillard tells us, is the most serious of crimes because it makes acts of obedience to the law and acts of transgression the same, canceling out the difference on which the law is based.[iv] The work of early burlesque performers embody Judith Butler's insistence that we "[c]onsider gender... as a corporeal style, an 'act,' as it were, which is both intentional and performative, where 'performative' suggests a dramatic and contingent construction of meaning."[v]

How, then, does all this relate to the practice of contemporary Gurlesque poetics? Take, for example, Danielle Pafunda's ventriloquization of a male character called "the fuckwad" in her poem "Advice Will Be Heeded Even As You Attempt To Head":

> The fuckwad says, my dear, my doughy dewy doe-eyed dimple,
> you mustn't attempt to think while you Sphinx. You
> mustn't leave the room now, for you haven't ever yet.
> And what will Odd Job think? What will he odious
> pus in the empty nest with a piddle of wire and a prong?

If her ventriloquization of "the fuckwad" seems ghastly, it is no less so than the female speaker's description of herself in the poem "I Am Now Your Own Private Spook Brigade":

Check me, fun wig candy spun ringlet red to ultra,
a peignoir smocked breast tattered ladder stitch ribbon
greased up hem, reflective glasses from the chop cop.
Nothing, though, 'til you see my stickware.

In these poems and others, Pafunda shows up the constructedness of gender through extreme hyperbole. What is unique about these ventriloquizations—and what marks Pafunda and other Gurlesque poets as Third rather than Second Wave feminists—is the simple fact that *these are not persona poems*. To engage in persona is to assume there is a face beneath the mask. Gurlesque poets, on the contrary, assume there is no such thing as coherent identity. There is no actual self, only the performance of self. This is one of several things that potentially separates Gurlesque poets from female Confessional or Neo-Confessional poets. For the Gurlesque poet, the use of the lyric "I" does not confess a self, but rather a raucously messy nest of conflicting desires and proclivities that can be costumed this way or that. Disjunctions in identity are not to be worked through or resolved but savored and tapped for their cultural power.[1]

"Love of the Unnatural": Artifice & Camp

The burlesque, of course, is closely related to the realm of camp. Susan Sontag, in her seminal essay "Notes on 'Camp'" writes, "the essence of Camp is the love of the unnatural: of artifice and exaggeration."[vi] And further, "Camp is a vision of the world in terms of style—but a particular kind of style. It is the love of the exaggerated, the 'off,' of things-being-what-they-are-not."[vii] Here, by way of

---

[1] This being said, it has never been clear to me that the poets we deem "confessional" actually conceive of their poetic practice as confession rather than the creation of a transitory, ephemeral self on the page. Sylvia Plath's hyper-performative poems, for example, have a far greater investment in a political performance of the female grotesque than in charting or transmitting any biographical information. Despite the singular sharpness of her voice, Plath's poems are interested in fictions that exceed and explode any concept of coherent self. Plath's keen sense of poem as artifice, like John Berryman's, appears deeply rooted in "self-as-performance," the node out of which Gurlesque poets are operating.

example, is an excerpt from Tina Celona's "Sunday Morning Cunt Poem":

> In my dream we were hitchhiking to Iowa City, but later when I looked at
> myself my cheeks were pink and so were my labia. Like a bird I discovered I
> had wings. I flew higher and higher, but when I got near the sun the wax
> melted and I fell into a poem by Auden. It was then that I wrote the poem
> "The Enormous Cock." For a while I hushed. Then I started up again about
> my cunt. Some said it was a vicious swipe at feminism. Others said it was a
> vicious feminist swipe. It was the only word I knew.

"To perceive Camp in objects and persons," writes Sontag, "is to understand
Being-as-Playing-a-Role. It is the farthest extension, in sensibility, of the
metaphor of life as theater."[viii] And while Sontag defines camp as an apolitical
sensibility, I propose that camp is rather the political posing as the apolitical, a
tactic that aims to make the reader complicit in the poem's political subtexts by
initially feigning that the poet's hyperbolic performance is nothing more than
self-parody. For the Gurlesque poet, all gender-inflected performance is essential-
ly "camping" and these performances are never divested of political subtexts.

In camp performance, the stress is on artifice. It is akin to Matei Calinescu's theo-
ry of kitsch as a form of semiotic ambiguity in which "objects are intended to
look both genuine and yet skillfully fake."[ix] This interest in artifice is one of the
hallmarks of Gurlesque poets who rail against classical canons of the Natural.
One of the many axioms of "the Natural" is the overplayed association of women
with the natural world, a trope in which women are allied with fauna and flora,
representing fecundity and a predilection to submit to masculine authority.
Ironically, women are also alleged to be "naturally" given over to the false and
artificial, given to make-up and costuming, to overvaluing useless trinkets, to
deceit. Listen to how poet Chelsey Minnis sets these convoluted terms and stereo-
types reeling in her poem "Uh," which begins:

> uh / I want to wear hot pants / and rest my boot on the back / of a
> man's neck / and / take a sharp cane / and / stick my heart / like / a
> piece of trash / in a park / and / rise out of arctic waters with curled ici-

cles in my hair and a speargun / and / buy a lazy game cat with claws /
that scratch me / and / uh! / someone should knock me down / and
press me against blue tile /and shuck / a gold sheath dress / off me /
and push / a shiny buzzer / to make me slide down a glistening chute

The way in which Minnis mobilizes various discourses against each other—
woman as petulant child, woman as monster, woman as inviting violence—is a
choice example of what Bakhtin calls "carnivalized writing."[x] The lush, often
kitschy imagery of Minnis's poem—hotpants and spearguns, leopard pillows and
cat-eye glasses—makes a parody of aesthetic consciousness, and yet it also forges
a new zone of consciousness, which is the poem itself. This is accomplished
through sheer stylistic overdetermination.

"From cosmos to cosmetics": Girly Kitsch

Theodor Adorno may have famously pronounced kitsch "the realm of artificial
imagery,"[xi] but other critics have been even more vituperative, calling kitsch a
parasite feeding on the production of "true art." Austrian novelist Hermann
Broch, an early theorist of kitsch, deplored Romanticism's "susceptibility to a dis-
astrous fall" from cosmic heights to kitsch: what Daniel Tiffany ironically calls
"a Luciferian swerve from cosmos to cosmetics." And the explosive dialectic
between specifically "girly kitsch" and masculine "high art" is one that
Gurlesque poets repeatedly exploit, recognizing that, as Tiffany puts it, kitsch's
resemblance to art "only enhances its catastrophically destructive challenge to the
[traditional] values of art."[xii]

The proper name for the domain of "girly kitsch" might be, in critic Sianne
Ngai's terms, the domain of "the Cute." While things cute may seem the least
harmful, least provocative of aesthetic categories, Ngai thinks otherwise. In "The
Cuteness of the Avant-Garde," Ngai suggests that violence lurks implicitly in the
aesthetic of "the Cute." Ngai notes, "the formal attributes associated with cute-
ness—smallness, compactness, softness, simplicity, and pliancy—call forth specif-
ic affects: helplessness, pitifulness, and even despondency."[xiv] And further, "in its
exaggerated passivity and vulnerability, the cute object is often intended to excite

a consumer's sadistic desires for mastery and control as much as his or her desire to cuddle."[xv]

Cuteness is, of course, the realm of pre-pubescent girls and their small, furry companions, and if cuteness speaks to an exaggerated difference in power—names an aesthetic encounter with a socially disempowered other[xvi]—the relationship of owner to captive pet is the relationship par excellence that illustrates this phenomenon. In Nada Gordon's flarfist poem "She Sure Likes the Cream, or The Pink Rabbits of Emilienne d'Alençon," an excess of cloying sweetness belies the S & M dialectic in which the aesthetic of cuteness is lodged, burrowing into the heart of the relationship between cuteness and violence:

> Sayonara fleurdelys.
> Adieu, cherry twinklemall.
> Human hair and glass EYES princess –
> mischief kreme.
>
> ...
>
> Come pet my kitty sweet kitty
> Yes, those with Empathy you like kitties
> you're nice you care Kitties are nice electric ferret
> DOES YOUR SWEET KITTY LOOK AT YOU LIKE THIS
> WHEN ASKED TO OBEY? My Little Kitty (40)

The preoccupation of pre-adolescent girls with all things cute, perhaps, speaks not to their attraction to things that mirror their own innocence but to things that mirror their own abjection and fear of further deformity ("human hair and glass EYES"); it reflects the degree to which they have already found themselves stripped of significant social agency. Cuteness, then, far from being a harmless aesthetic category, reveals a state of acute deformity.

The Female Grotesque & the Aesthetics of Contamination

Make no mistake, though: there is a palpable quest for pleasure at the heart of this excessive poetics, an utter delight in the grotesque. As Arielle Greenberg noted in her original talk on the Gurlesque given at Small Press Traffic in 2002, "[The] honest assessment of the perverse pleasures of horror—even horror so closely associated with women's suppression—is one of the key markers of the Gurlesque." The Gurlesque's appropriation of the grotesque, like its appropriation of burlesque, camp, and kitsch, stands in outright defiance of classical aesthetics and their masculocentric practices. If the burlesque is always about the body on display (i.e. the gendered surface of the body), the grotesque engages the body as a biological organism. To Bakhtin, women represent the quintessential grotesque: they are "penetrable, suffer the addition of alien body parts, and become alternately huge and tiny."[xvii] Grotesque bodies, male or female, are no longer "clearly differentiated from the world but transferred, merged, fused with it."[xviii] Mary Russo writes,

> The images of the grotesque body are precisely those which are abjected from bodily canons of classical aesthetics. The classical body is transcendental and monumental, closed, static, self-contained, symmetrical and sleek; it is identified with "high" or official culture... with the rationalism, individualism, and the normalizing aspirations of the bourgeoisie. The grotesque body is open, protruding, irregular, secreting, multiple, and changing; it is identified with non-official "low" culture..., and with social transformation.[xix]

In Gurlesque poetry, human bodies and human language (and thus identity) are not closed, discrete systems. They are grotesque bodies/systems—never finished, ever-morphing, unstable, and porous. The body, as the nexus of language and identity, is a strange borderland, the site of erratic and highly specific (and language-mediated) desires. Here is an excerpt of Ariana Reines' "Dear Marguerite":

I want a world to live in. I want a world to live in and I am vomiting cause there is no world. There are vessels that have had their innards emptied out, sliding around in the lube. Boinking her potato face with his thick stuff and she put a disease on his meat so it oozes green.

In Reines' poetic schema, we are all slaughterhouse animals, "vessels that have had their innards emptied out." Grotesque bodies also abound in Cathy Park Hong's poetry, which vocalizes a monstrous "not-belongingness." In her two books, female multilingual speakers are stranded between languages and diverging cultural views on how they, as women, are expected to behave. In "Zoo," for example, the speaker's descriptions of her own body are disturbingly inflected with a racist and sexist critique that has been deeply internalized, offering up "a mute girl with the baboon's face" and "piscine skin," who speaks in a "voice like the flash of bats" or "hyena babble" or "apish libretto."

In Hong's poems, there is no experience of "pure" culture or language available to us, no "pure" identity, no unmediated desire. The concept of the pure lies at the heart of Western aesthetics—the word "catharsis" comes from the Greek verb "to purify"—and women, non-whites, queers, impoverished, or disabled persons have historically been labeled as social contaminants. Gurlesque poets deny catharsis because they deny the aesthetics of the pure.

The Quest for Female Pleasure

While the grotesque may seem a radical aesthetic, what is perhaps even more radical is Gurlesque poets' insistence on placing female pleasure at the center of their poetics. bell hooks has repeatedly critiqued Second Wave feminists for seeing their desire for political change as a separate entity from the longings and passions that are the stuff of their everyday lives. The desire for radical social change, hooks asserts, is intimately linked with the desire for pleasure and erotic fulfillment.[xx] With a nod to hooks (and writers like Gertrude Stein), Gurlesque poets put the unabashed quest for female pleasure at the center of their poetics. This, along with their disavowal of persona, is one of the primary things that separates them from poets of earlier generations, such as Sylvia Plath.

In Plath's "Lady Lazarus," for example, the speaker is performing a female burlesque, a "strip tease," that ultimately "unwraps" the female body not as an erotic object but the site of grotesque mortality and non-compliant subjectivity. The speaker ironically wields her body as a souvenir of her own death-drive, both performing and mocking the idea of souvenir as a trace of authentic experience. Yet by the end of the poem, as in so many of Plath's poems, the speaker feels compelled to disembody herself. This stands in stark contrast to Gurlesque poets, who insist on the multiple pleasures of female embodiment. As Cathy Wagner quips: "I'm total I'm all I'm absorbed in this *meat cake*."[2] Compare Plath's famous "Fever 103°"—which conflates illness and physical ecstasy and ends, once again, with her "selves dissolving"—to an excerpt from Wagner's long sequence "Imitating":

My greed was outrageous
power-outageous
I felt all better & feverish
My braincase was
hypertranslucent

. . .

I was mine & I was going
To dig myself a jewel.
I dug a little bone in me
I dug a little boneshaped
hole in me, I loved it
Hello you fuckers!
Dug around in there making
    my emergencies go off
I thought they were lovebells
    or runaway truck ramps

---

[2] *Meat cake*, by the way, is also the name of Dame Darcy's comic series begun in the early 1990s, several images of which are reproduced in this anthology.

I'm hungry.

The speaker in this poem ranges between one corporeal craving and another, unfazed by the "emergencies" of ecstatic experience. Nor does she feel the need to call herself a "whore," as Plath does in "Fever 103°." Despite these contrasts, it must be acknowledged that Plath was one of the first poets to understand the risks of female self-display in poetry. It is simply not possible for a female poet to claim, like Whitman, that she intends to "go by the bank of the wood and become undisguised and naked" without immediately becoming vulnerable to the male gaze. It is, in fact, very difficult for female poets to speak of their embodied experience without being misread as positioning themselves as erotic objects.

In Wagner's poem and elsewhere, Gurlesque poets are deploying an aesthetics of spectacle. The staging of spectacle, as theorists such as Walter Benjamin and Guy Debord have noted, is invariably motivated by a political agenda; engaging in spectacle inevitably risks the aestheticization of politics and, even more problematic, the aestheticization of violence. The Gurlesque's relationship to violence is deliberately ambiguous: while condemning barbarity, many of these poets draw on destructive energies to perform their social critique. Their work swerves between parodies of violence to its enactment, which, in the hands of women, becomes strikingly transgressive. Gurlesque poetry thus investigates the collision/collusion of fantasy and ethics at the core of Western cultural battles.

A Gurlesque Genealogy

Like the riot grrls that preceded them, Gurlesque poets enact signs, bodies and psyches in crisis, and do so by making the spectator complicit in their crisis. The minor miracle is that these poets do so with such provocative humor and a great degree of pleasure. Their tactics, however, are not without precedent. Their ambiguous relationship to violence, for example, draws on the energies of Berlin Dada and other avant-gardes. Speaking broadly, Gurlesque poets inherit from the historical avant-garde a suspicion of the arts and culture industry as being complicit with the aims of capitalism and imperialism, as well as a simultaneous love of the bedazzling ephemera thrown off by high capitalist culture.

More specifically, Gurlesque poets inherit Baudelaire's quarrel with mimesis as the foundational principle of art and Rimbaud's interest in mongrel identity. They inherit Mina Loy's provocative humor and her interest in the female abject, Gertrude Stein's insistence on female pleasure, Djuna Barnes' baroque eroticism, and Marianne Moore's sense of the self as a curated collection. With Baroness Else von Freytag, the New York Dadaist poet and proto-punk performance artist, they share an interest in aggressively deconstructing female rituals of self-display and the libidinal economies that encourage/depend on them.[3] From male Modernists and avant-gardists, they inherit Marcel Duchamp's gender-bending antics and an interest in deconstructing the male gaze, as well as early T. S. Eliot's productive use of gender instability. Gurlesque poets also share Russian Futurist Vladimir Mayakovsky's use of camp to unseat gender binaries, a mode of performance that was later revived by Frank O'Hara.

In addition to O'Hara's use of camp, Gurlesque poets owe much to other mid-century poets: Plath's engagement with the female grotesque and her ambiguous, politically loaded self-display; John Berryman's performative externalization of social violence ("We are using our own skins for wallpaper"); Anne Sexton's inability to respond to repeated insistence that she tone down the explicitly female content of her poems; Amiri Baraka's sense of the biological body as the limit of the collective social body; Lucille Clifton's revelation that "There is a girl inside / She is randy as a wolf."

More recently, Gurlesque tendencies can be located in the work of Kathy Acker, Alice Notley, and Dodie Bellamy, all of whom have an express interest in subverting masculine forms. Gurlesque poets also draw, knowingly or unknowingly, on the work of contemporary theorists, including those mentioned above (Ngai,

---

[3]Those who came across the Baroness, whether in the New York streets or in highbrow salons, were invariably nonplussed by this woman who shaved her head and painted it vermillion, or sported two tomato cans as a bra, or hung spoons from her ears as earrings, who wore a coal scuttle as a hat, or a bird cage as a necklace (with a live canary inside). For a number of years, Wallace Stevens admitted to being afraid to venture south of 14th St. for fear of coming across her.

Butler), as well as Julia Kristeva's work on abjection, Judith Halberstam's work on the monster as a cultural object, and Donna Haraway's work on hybrid bodies. And lastly – need I even say it? – Gurlesque poets clearly owe a great debt to Emily Dickinson, the original Goth girl.

I am not insisting that this genealogy forms a common knowledge base for Gurlesque poets; the poets in this anthology may claim few or none of these writers as influences, and each certainly has a rich genealogical tree of their own to offer. I intend the above merely as a loose sketch of aesthetic tendencies and impulses, an artistic and theoretical heritage from which the Gurlesque draws its manifold, relentless energies.

—Lara Glenum, 2009

Notes:
[i]Robert C. Allen, Horrible Prettiness: Burlesque and American Culture (Chapel Hill: University of North Carolina Press, 1991), 29.
[ii]Loose Women in Tights: Images of Femininity in Early Burlesque Performance, ed. Emily Layne Fargo, Ohio State University Online Exhibition, 1 September 2008,
<http://library.osu.edu/sites/exhibits/burlesque>
[iii]Allen, 25.
[iv]Jean Baudrillard,. Simulacra and Simulation. (Ann Arbor: The University of Michigan Press, 1995) 21.
[v]Judith Butler, The Judith Butler Reader, ed. Sara Salih (Boston: Blackwell Publishing, 2004), 113.
[vi]Susan Sontag, Against Interpretation (New York: Picador, 2001), 275.
[vii]Sontag, 279.
[viii]Sontag, 280.
[ix]Matei Calinescu, Five Faces of Modernity (Durham: Duke University Press, 1987), 252.
[x]Mikhail Bakhtin, Rabelais and his World, trans. Helene Iswolsky (Cambridge: MIT, 1968), 19.
[xi]Theodor Adorno, "Veblen's Attack on Culture," Studies in Philosophy and Social Science 9 (1941): 401.
[xii]Daniel Tiffany, "Kitsching The Cantos," Modernism/modernity 12.2 (April 2005): 329.
[xiii]Tiffany, 320.
[xiv]Sianne Ngai, "The Cuteness of the Avant-Garde," Critical Inquiry 31.4 (Summer 2005): 816.
[xv]Ibid.
[xvi]Ngai, 828.
[xvii]Bakhtin, 339.

xviiiIbid.

xixMary Russo, The Female Grotesque: Risk, Excess and Modernity (New York: Routledge, 1994), 8.

xxhooks, bell, Reel to Real: Race, Sex, and Class at the Movies (New York: Routledge, 1996), 29.

ARIANA REINES

BLOWHOLE

Because of remembering where or what you are the ovum gasp and burst. First he spit on my asshole and then start in with a middle finger and then the cock slid in no sound come out, only a maw gaping, grind hard into ground. Voluminous bounty of minutes sensate and glowing shoot out.

SHE say when she drink liquid it leak into her sinuses. HE grinding his stuff with his hand. SHE refusing operation. SHE want him to have murder her. So he BROKE her eyes she face brain. A day exist so I can not think.

Liquid shoot into her skull and leak out her eye hole.

Thick book like his fat head when I sit on it and fart. All kinds signification room for all. Moistest mouth is cow's mouth sorrow face normal. Hung up hund legs reversed negated shit brains inside rear world.

ANTHEM

I am a mart in the dog, and look, here's some merchandise. I am a mart in the dog. Aye.

Being a mart in a dog is like being a world: overstated.

Do you know what love is if you are a mart in a dog. You sell Hoodsies and cigarettes and lotto tickets. You are real.

Do you know what a dog is if you are trapped inside of him.

Everything is part of something.

I am part of something because my life is so stupid.

Being a mousse made of stars in the night that I want to feel is being too because I am gluey like a girl.

I even am a girl. Wow, fuck me.

Being a night inside of the mouth of a loved boy. Red black and shiny teeth with a tongue. The word of a loved boy has sense.

In a mart where there are newspapers and burnt coffee all the night long, bic pens in a jar, scratch tickets and pornography, everything's ok. I am not the nice man in the mart I am the mart itself, which is inside of a dog who could love me by instinct except he doesn't know I am inside of him and a mart isn't an I.

Infinity has got to become mine so that I can know which way to turn, so that I can know in what direction something like morning is breaking.

I LOVE MY EMERGENCY

An alabaster fidget is impossible to imagine
Nevertheless they spent a long time wanting to fuck statues
And having hair that didn't move when a wave came.

The wave rises to a point and pierces the moon.
It is night. I have a jaw which could be a gunwale.
I have the night which is a hemp cord in my hard hand.

Nobody fucking understands, when the building coughed up the white
Rubble of everything, whitening us with its dust. A little blood on our lips
We were the real's dead mimes. Or stained minutes.

This is a permanent poem. If I don't fuck today I'll die.
This is a poem the size of almost nothing: a blotter made rude
By its inexorable silkening.

A wobble ate canned pie filling and, like the centuries,
Grew into an angry augur.
All time is a piece of shit, nothing but a warning.

FATED

I am the bride of my baby. I am the bride of this ok day. The sun is a peeled yolk. I broke.

I = Miss Havisham. Combustion heaven. To be changed, to go up up up, to be translated. HOW DO THE BEASTS GROAN! THE HERDS OF CATTLE ARE PERPLEXED, BECAUSE THEY HAVE NO PASTURE, YEA, THE FLOCKS OF SHEEP ARE MADE DESOLATE

I hate you therefore we will be together forever, slice me open if I ever smooth this over, slice me open if I ever soften, if I ever moisten, if I ever fall for you again

VALVE

How come she has got to die before I can really have her.
Cuz in heat she used to become other than what she had assimilated.
Delve into the marzipan of her rutted teats.
You have got to squeeze her squeeze her squeeze her
VALVE
I was stupid enough to put my mouth on his round mouth. Every O is if not a
Messiah then seems a future. Mwa. Tongue cut my heart out because it does
worse than love, it talks
VALVE
My Warsawa got so hot. He wasn't going even to try to love me. Oh pooches,
need me! Up her ass a maggot smelling of leather and amber and hair, Baudelaire.
What does a country need a poet for. To put bunting up on the dead shanks of
dreams
VALVE
His thick thick in my Warsawa. So basically you peel the skin off and slice the
thing in half with a chainsaw, vertically. Every man wants to groom me split me
open I wish
VALVE
My Warsawa lost her way drownded in the River Bug. Harpists with hair long
strands of brown fish shit. Downloaded today's sugar and the thick one wants to
know if I'm coming over only if this muscle can force feel
VALVE
Spackles the info bits. Language is the kind of failure inside of which you learn to
fall in love. Much of her giant digestion has to do with metaphor or is it, is its
essence. I don't care about my sorrow anymore because I and the minors who
used to be me are not curable. Giantessa, hide me
VALVE
Hide
VALVE

EARMARK

She clasped the event to her and proceeded. Fucked her steaming eyehole and ended it. The cracked thing was a doomed pidgin, it meant something

Yesterday. A patience would be ideal. Make an art of it, sere notes winding their way through an air to have become the name of her going. Her name on the list, and some certain information they had.

After a time there is no more accuracy, after a time you can't get the note clean of what it might have been.

Under the skirt of mother ginger huddle little boys and girls. A holiday shit stain. His scholarliness justifies those flights

Of fancy you condemn in him. And the gummy hulls of words muzzle the chaw, a kind of cud that will not do. An umlaut could be a cousin's bone.

The poisoned nuance that started everything. It was from eating ourselves. It had to be

Someone else's sickness first, our silence, our good balance, our usefulness. There is something certain creatures long for. To be hacked up and macerated. That's coming out and go into another body.

Eaten, gemmed with grease and herbs. Whose low language ruined our bowels. Whose lowing even meant nothing. We knew we were to become a ream of flesh. Another nothing.

AND BLINDLY WE FOREFEEL

A roof's invaginated ornaments, the lowing of the dark cattle under a stand of air.

I then you pluck the procession out according to the text that prescribed it.

We know it must be better than what we can say for it.

We know our intelligence will betray the clits of sorrow that shudder and jerk off the last of day.

We don't care we don't care we don't care.

A bolus of words passing from one world into the next, sourer and sourer, worse and worse, aloner. Mooted,

Rent, rubbered, hated, ended, ended.

DOCUMENTARY POETRY

Two sylphs trying to climb down off a note
Are nothing for the mystery of their exteriority.
Moo goo gai pan equals the sunset and slowly
But surely my girl's brain is the universe.
This is the best chic drek of the puppy day.
The final feeling of slow learners rounding a bend.

This is the best of two wombs competing for one hot stay.
It's the wobble her expriation looks like, which
Is a booboo ruining the tragedy she prepared for it.
He wants to be more culpable than me.
We wear the war, shoot the piano, fuck her panties, bleach
The bright chromes, and a sun slavers over hairs and woofers
And the lady's cracks cleave to her nightie just as hipster bitches get tanked
Ruin their makeup and fuck sobbing and bareassed on the sidewalk
Bleeding bad air and sorrel, slashing their perfect tits, getting carded
The usual taxation, no fun, self-confidence, worse than nerd boners etc
And no hand comes to pierce the perfect night

KNOCKER

Acres of wishes inside her. Any liver. To harden the gut. Boys rinse their arms in what falls from my carotid. My body is the opposite of my body when they hang me up by my hind legs. I mean the opposite thing. I guess this is about identity. Not becoming animal. Not a wall with windows in it and flaglets of laundry waving or being so easy to mouth his so-thick. Sloes and divorcing her miserable eyes from the rumor they stir up in me. Everything on the planet is diverted.

Worse is less bloody pussies to lick. Everything good's an animal.

Asymptomatic. Causing one thing to fuck another. Introducing between one thing and another one of those copula that is an and. Genitals are for togetherness. Put her two feet in the stirrups.

I wish I could remember when it was her mouth fastened itself in the rictus of pure hunger she still wears. Her teeth the color of some kind of caviar or dirty marble, shining behind the waxen smear of mouth. I don't care what happens next except to see her. I don't want to know the end of the story.

So skyey guilty for existing. Light's a kind of bane. Fish fat. Factota. I need that man in my life.

In heat a lady could be other than what she had assimilated. Two breasts of almond paste. She smiled against the cracked varnish on her mouth. Pates basted in sunshine. Or whole instances of consciousness corralled inside themselves. What's the outermost border of a thought, what's the ordure of an event. In heat a lady. Tits swinging like white udders, engorgèd apertures. Woman make me. Want to be a jockstrap, shit-stained. Walled-in by her own substance. A car encased her or an agate. Steamships and pissoirs, the resinous accretion of pharmaceuticals in her. Antimacassars embroidered with zodiacs, gold threads, incisors, or womb. A little everyday renovation.

IN THE EVENING TOZAN SWAM AROUND IN A SEA OF GOOD AND BAD, BUT AT DAWN UMMON CRUSHED HIS NUT SHELL

I put my panties on.

Also I do not care for panties but I put my hand in them.

A villanelle does not make me feel better about my life.

This lad is a nice lad; look, he stands his pals for a round.

A man pinched my nipple because we were in the lobby of the Algonquin Hotel.

I do not know this man before our first meeting during which he pinches my nipple
        because I do not mind.

This is a difficult life but it is not the most difficult. It will make me die.

Anna Nicole Smith died.

Why did you say that the star fell and melted like an ice cube into some wood. That
        had nothing to do with it.

I did not know if there was anybody to talk to but I did not think that there was
        because I succeeded in talking and there
            was approbation in the air, haha, and nevertheless we did not seem to know
        each other after the talking was over.

The Asian girl, this is interesting, grooms her kooch so that it looks like a strip of
        electrical tape.

The correct answer is to fold a sheet of looseleaf paper in half and stand it up. This
        stands for every aspect of a day.

The adulthood of the talented people is not so interesting.

Next I can not describe the grit inside of the conventionally-grown peach which is
        capable of burning the roof of the mouth but the peach is large and is
        not largeness a kind of satisfaction, yes it is.

Nevertheless he cannot get past his individual intelligence.

But the shadows proceed, like a long, slow scrawl.

Some ejaculate does taste like celery, yes. However literature does not taste like anything.

from **COEUR DE LION**

You are writing a book called *Mein Cock*.

It is about your love affair

With a phone sex operator, among other things.

When you told me the story of you

And the phone sex operator

I was moved. After you read

Me about fifty pages of your novel, *Humble*

Monster, and I told you it was "a terrible novel"

(I did not mean to say it like that)

I explained some things

That I did like about it, some things

I thought could be reworked. And

I said that I hoped

That you could write the story

Of you and the phone-sex operator

How good she was at cocksucking

How shitty her life

Was, her poverty, fucked-up

Family, how she hated her

Body, the love you shared.

I felt for her, and you spoke

About her with such elegant

Forthrightness.

The week after school ended

And I was in Germany with Sinan

I got obsessed with Nazi architecture

And started to read *Mein Kampf* online

Until I got blocked by the authorities.

I told you all about it in an e-mail

On August 30th and I feel

That perhaps I am somewhere in some

Small way a part of what has inspired

You to write this book *Mein Cock*.

On the other hand, I think your prose

Is sometimes shaky, and following Hitler's

Might not be the best idea.

I guess "cock" could stand

For *kampf*, "struggle," which is pretty

Witty, or could be, but who knows

Where you're going to go with

That. It's really none of my business.

BRENDA COULTAS

DREAM LIFE IN A CASE OF TRANSVESTISM

1.

I'm in a man's uniform with military creases in the shirt. I search an informant for drugs or money, to verify that she goes in clean. It's very hot. She wears a tank top, shorts, and slip-on shoes. She pulls up her top; nothing beneath her breasts but a wire taped on for sound. I look down her shorts, pubic hair shaved. Check inside the soles of her shoes. Nothing. It's daylight and we are in an empty railroad yard.

2.

My sister and I walk down the midway in matching sailor suits. My cousin Tommy is dressed in a nautical jacket, carrying a cane with a ceramic dalmatian head. All the carnie barkers watch. They wish they were dressed like us.

3.

At a party for girls only, I wear a can-can dress with big kittens on the skirt. It has a velcro zipper that I like to open and close. We take our clothes off. They all turn out to be boys. Later, I found out that I went on the wrong day.

4.

I am a woman dressed as a man dressed as a woman. I am so much a woman I do not recognize myself. Yet I have never been more of a man.

My testicles lie beneath my skin and I touch the two knots in my groin. When I swear I place my right hand upon them and tell the truth, as told by me, a liar.

5.

Since I became a women dressed as a man dressed as a women, I lost my virginity. There are sixteen types of hymens. I had thirteen of them. My hymen was a chameleon that hung from a chain on my sweater and changed shaped constantly.

"What is that on your sweater?"

"Its just an old maidenhead that I spray painted gold and glued some sequins onto."

6.

I lost it in a car in Kentucky, beneath the bridge where I was born in the car's back seat. My father drove, the doctor in back with my mother. My father drove faster and faster. Her pains came closer and closer together. The crown of my head emerged. We were late crossing the water. All of us were very, very

late.
MARGARET

Every day, Margaret and her monkey go to the baby show to look for Margaret's daughter. The monkey is on a leash and very well trained. He is not allowed to touch any glass.

Hanging on the outside of the show tent are paintings of the babies: the cyclops child, the lamb-headed boy, the twins joined at the waist, the lizard-faced girl.

The paintings are large and bright.

The show is owned by two men who are lovers. Every day the female one dusts the jars and checks their fluid levels. They live in a trailer behind the tent. The trailer is full of small dogs they breed to sell.

Margaret dances in The Arabian Nights show. She stands on a platform at show time and shimmies in her harem outfit, made of chiffon veils and lined with gold coins. Her monkey rides on her shoulders and unhooks the colored layers during her dance.

Margaret stares at the baby jars and wonders if one of them were taken out, would her or she be rubbery like a rotten egg. The babies' faces are pressed up against the glass. In the bigger jars, some of them float up to the trop as if to take a breath and then dive to the bottom.

Sometimes pieces break off of the older ones and sink to the bottom. The men use a long handled spoon to scoop up the fragments.

Margaret's lover is Mike the Mouse. He entices the marks to play. He says, "Come on in and win you one, come on in and win."

The mice are all white and come from a pet store. He uses one per night. The mouse runs into a numbered hole, sometimes it is stunned. He shakes a stick at it until it moves.

The prizes are stuffed animals.

On their mattress, in the bed of the hoochie-coochie wagon, he says to Margaret, "Come on in and win."

Each tear-down night, the two men pack the jars between newspapers to cushion the ride. They roll up the canvas and everything folds in upon itself.

Sometimes Margaret sees a new one or notices one in the back behind the other jars. She wonders where all the babies come from.

Her own baby was a lion-faced girl with a split lip that curled up on the edges. The doctor showed her and took the girl away.

The father was Arlo the gypsy boy. He lived in a trailer with his family. All the children slept on cots outside. He was the milk bottle man. He said, "Knock 'em over and win. Knock 'em over and win."

No one could knock the bottles down. They were filled with weights.

He said to Margaret in the top booth of the empty grandstand, "You knock me over."

Margaret wears a dress made of mirrors. She's a tourist attraction; a reflecting

pool of human wonder.
THE SHED

Directions. This is a very easy film to make as the hogs are predictable in their behavior and limited in range by the pen; however, they are deceased, and I took part in eating them, thus this is a most difficult film to make. Build a three-room shed out of wood with a tin roof and flat head nails. Plant thistles and pigweed. Dig a wallow and fill with water.

Narrative: The pig shed is gone and where it stood are green grasses. A neighbor bought half of the land and put up a stable of goats (says they are the main ingredient in pepperoni). I can remember our pigs without the aid of hypnosis or memory drugs. There's Pearl, the mama. Rusty with his reddish patches (my pig), and Dogfood (Peggy's pig).
Can you capture the sound of my hog call?
We stocked the wallow with tadpoles, who died despite our efforts.

Film us (four girls) in the wallow, deepening the hole.

Can you film us thinking "If we could only float a boat in here then we would truly have everything: water, mud and navigation?"

Shoot a closeup of nose rings and film us scraping our plates into a coffee can, turning dinner into hog slop. Can you film the ghost of Pearl? Pan out to the humans, on bicycles and foot, rooting in junkyards on the old Moore place, rooting in ravines full of abandoned cars.

I try to ride my pig but fall off. I pet my pig. Lay my head down on his rump. I am a small human, so small that my underpants come up to my armpits. Buster Weatherholt's dog, Old Blue, always sat down when I tried to ride him. I sat on his back, then he sat down on hind legs and I slid off.

We wanted machines or animals for transport: swings, merry go rounds and maypoles for flying. We tried to ride everything our size, living or not. Ponies were too high up. We considered a wooden wagon with wooden wheels, we could take to the prairies in this, but we need a team. I dreamed of so many treasures buried in the earth or of just bones, all the bones buried by time, nature or natives.

Given eternity, we could find marvelous bones.

II

from "A SUMMER NEWSREEL"

This is the almost last summer of this century in a town where our streets, laid out in 1876, were left off the late 20th century surveyor's map.

Why am I writing about maps when Indiana is bursting beneath my feet stained purple with mulberries?

The crickets hum louder than the TV. Father's oxygen sounds like running water, like a stream. Stream o' life for him. He sits or lies down.

Brenda sorts through boxes in the attic.
Mom plants a flower.
The dogs sleep under the car.
The cats breed and kill.

As for the Coultas you can take them or leave em. They either get skinnier or chunky at mid-life. As for them, well, they'd rather be left out of any poem.

So many would like to be Brenda Coultas, chewing and stripping tobacco like a grasshopper.

So many people would like to be her, making taffy all summer and living near Holiday World where everyday is a holiday. So many would love be her at the drive-in with 6 screens and her own car. So many of you would like to be me with your own car.

At the Rockport cemetery stands a headstone shaped like a horse. An entire horse, not a horse bust or just horse penis but the full body of my cousin who fucked a girl there in the cemetery. A living girl on a blanket that she carried in her car, and now I pause to think of the horse.

What will the Coultas family do today? Mom will fry bacon. Dad will work a
crossword puzzle. The entire family will mow again and plant one mum.

For so many, I'm going to do today what they wish they could do for themselves.
Breathing
walking
driving
eating
turning on lights & growing turnips.

Is there something that you would like me to do today?
Is there something Brenda Coultas can do for you? She would like to help you.
She is reading and writing and stopping to serve you. Everyone is robed in
burlap. Brenda Coultas covered you in quilts while you were singing.

BRENDA SHAUGHNESSY

YOUR ONE GOOD DRESS

should never be light. That kind of thing
feels like a hundred shiny-headed waifs backlit
and skeletal, approaching. Dripping and in
unison, murmuring, "We are you."

No. And the red dress (think about it,
redress) is all neckhole. The brown
is a big wet beard with, of course, a
backslit. You're only as sick as your secrets.

There is an argument for the dull-chic,
the dirty olive and the Cinderelly. But
those who exhort it are only part of the conspiracy:
"Shimmer, shmimmer," they'll say. "Lush, shmush."

Do not listen. It's a part of the anti-obvious
movement and it's sheer matricide. Ask your
mum. It would kill her if you were ewe gee el why.
And is it a crime to wonder, am I. In the dark a dare,

Am I now. You put on your Niña, your Pinta,
your Santa María. Make it simple to last your whole
life long. Make it black. Glassy or deep.
Your body is opium and you are its only true smoker.

This black dress is your one good dress.
Bury your children in it. Visit your pokey
hometown friends in it. Go missing for days.
Taking it off never matters. That just wears you down.

DEAR GONGLYA,

The most inscrutable beautiful names in this world
always do sound like diseases.
It is because they are engorged.
G., I am a fool.
What we feel in the solar plexus wrecks us.
Halfway squatting on a crate where feeling happened. Caresses.

You know corporeal gifts besmirch thieves like me.
But she plucks a feather and my steam escapes.
                                        We're awake
each night at pennymoon and we micro and necro.
I can't stop. But love and what-all:
the uncomfortable position of telling the truth,
like the lotus, can't be held long.
                            If she knew would she
just take all her favors from my marmalade
vessel and chuck them back
into the endless reversible garment which is my life—
                            an astonishing vanishing.
G., I know this letter is like a slice of elevator accident.
As smart folk would say,
"Everything is only Nothing's Truck."

I would revise it and say that everything is only
nothing, truncated.

Love,

Your Igor

ARACHNOLESCENCE

I see I have so quickly endeared you to my dazzled fray
of bedpan. With a stealth hand on my breastbone,
I've pilfered the last gangrene remedy, honey-wax fiber,
from my neighbor all century and I've bullied you
into a few cramps yourself. Give me drug
of terrifying strength or I will become it.

Love me in my strict empire of phantom pain,
in my wiliest contempt for all that is mere fever
and sweat, strain and maculate, florid and maternal,
decent and plain. I want theater, the domain
of intoxicated grief. And spifflicated louts are we,
absolute gourmands of the ugliest meal.

I have a radium of the soul, a petulant amputation, eight!
A poultice for you, my arachno-demigod, wacky and skeptical
A promise of loot and skulduggery for all your children.

I've won the tourniquet, I've devastated toddlers
in the height of their podlike fashion, in their pink-
naped heaven of Erasmus and his near-wife, Chlamydia.
Give me five years, lovers, I will give you the ancient
torture device constructed of kisses, in the glum transfusion
of crisp, lichen climate with rectangular erotics.

I will kill you with the blistering foods of a Crimean war,
sluiced with a dura mater's soldier-ration of tiny
moistures, in this temple of my tryst with the daughter
of the red god's red dog. I will solder you to the Krsna
of ironworks and most bellicose dementia. Give me
liberty or give me everything you've ever loved.

Stop me, my ancient history, as you always have,
before I poison my own sleep with the wanderlust
of this my stardom in the galaxy of worms and toxic ability.

PARTHENOGENESIS

It's easy to make more of myself by eating,
and sometimes easy's the thing.

To be double-me, half the trouble
but not lonely.

Making cakes to celebrate any old day.
Eating too much: the emperor of being used.

Nature, mature and feminized,
naturalizes me naturally by creating

the feeling of being a natural woman,
like a sixteen-year-old getting knocked up

again. To solve that problem,
there's the crispness of not eating,

a pane of glass with a bloody-edged
body, that is, having the baby at the prom

undetected and, in a trance of self-preservation,
throwing it away in the girls' room trash.

Buried under paper towels, silent.
Nothing could be better, for the teenager.

For me, starving, that coreless, useful feeling,
is not making myself smaller

but making myself bigger, inside.
It's prince and pauper both, it's starving artist

and good model in one masterpiece.
It rhymes with *marveling* and that's no accident

Fullness is dullness. Dreaming's too easy.
But sometimes I don't care.

Sometimes I put in just the right amount,
but then I'm the worst kind of patsy, a chump

giving myself over to myself like a criminal
to the law, with nothing to show for it.

No reward, no news, no truth.
It's too sad to be so ordinary every day.

Like some kind of employee.
Being told what to do. Chop off a finger

to plant in fertilizer (that is, in used animal
food), to grow a finger tree.

More fingers for me. Stop saying *finger*.
I'm the one in charge here.

Stop the madness and just eat the mirror.
Put it in sideways or crush it

into a powder. It doesn't hurt and it works.
Mouth full, don't talk.

Nothing to say. I'll be a whole new person.
I'll make her myself. Then we'll walk away.

We'll say to each other how she's changed.
How we wouldn't have recognized us.

FIRST DATE AND STILL VERY, VERY LONELY

A pleasant, leather poison
is the trick to smelling
good to female saddles,

that is, saddles with a hole
and not a pommel. Remember
those? Gone the way

of vestal virgins and tight
white black holy hell and with it
the lesbian Elysium of old.

I miss the idea of wives.
The loving circle.
But onward. Today

is a sacred day. A date day.
An exception to the usual
poor me, poor me!

I'm not poor and I'm not me.
I remember both
states as soon ago as last week.

But that's history.
This is different. At a party,
once, everyone was so careful

that only I cut my lip drinking
from the winterspring,
a kind of cold, decorative trough

centerpiece we were all
drinking from. The idea is
you're like animals.

If you ask, about the cut, *Why me?*
The answer is, *Of course me.*
In what world ever possible not me?

I could admit that with open blood
running down my chin
like hyena butter or gasoline.

I was mortified, really lost.
After that I thought,
I have to meet someone.

I'M OVER THE MOON

I don't like what the moon is supposed to do.
Confuse me, ovulate me,

spoon-feed me longing. A kind of ancient
date-rape drug. So I'll howl at you, moon,

I'm angry. I'll take back the night. Using me to
swoon at your questionable light,

you had me chasing you,
the world's worst lover, over and over

hoping for a mirror, a whisper, insight.
But you disappear for nights on end

with all my erotic mysteries
and my entire unconscious mind.

How long do I try to get water from a stone?
It's like having a bad boyfriend in a good band.

Better off alone. I'm going to write hard
and fast into you, moon, face-fucking.

Something you wouldn't understand.
You with no swampy sexual

promise but what we glue onto you.
That's not real. You have no begging

cunt. No panties ripped off and the crotch

sucked. No lacerating spasms

sending electrical sparks through the toes.
Stars have those.

What do you have? You're a tool, moon.
Now, noon. There's a hero.

The obvious sun, no bullshit, the enemy
of poets and lovers, sleepers and creatures.

But my lovers have never been able to read
my mind. I've had to learn to be direct

It's hard to learn that, hard to do.
The sun is worth ten of you.

You don't hold a candle
to that complexity, that solid craze.

Like an animal carcass on the road at night,
picked at by crows,

haunting walkers and drivers. Your face
regularly sliced up by the moving

frames of car windows. Your light is drawn,
quartered, your dreams are stolen.

You change shape and turn away,
letting night solve all night's problems alone.

CATHERINE WAGNER

THIS IS A FUCKING POEM

don't expect too much.

Well I expect you to go into the
fucking human tunnel
I'm going.

pink grimy glossed
entabulature, welted
and tattooed. Enfolded in
ropy ceiling-hangings
but it isn't a room,

and bumblingly sliding
out, little legs of

a little girl, bum on the wall/opening

pink legs sticking out like a
hermit crab's, she's coming!

shudder out the little-girl
legs with a little
girl head mostly eyes, no ears,
bug brain, aimless

Send her to school

It's cold, and where should she
go, she will eat her

legs with her mandibles

her eyes will retract inside.

Stroke her riding hood
Settle down, little

nobody will hurtcha

by breaking off your little legs,
six little legs,
if you come.

COMING AND I DID NOT RUN AWAY

STILL not finished review
but productive day and feeling
    GÜT
like a fine mama
    SHÜT
putting down some
    RÜTS
like the lost queen
    TOOT
    TOOT
    TÜT TÜT TÜT
Brand spankin hanky pankin
 new periodical
   in my uterus
       yest I cried
       thought I was going
       NÜTSO
Not So   Ah so? yes it was just

a periodical
making me illogical
not wrong though
I was not wrong

I saw the "usual turn of phrase"
coming and I did not run away
I lay around
Webby tree
Please do to me

CAFÉ ROUGE

Inside of cage thing
Spreading wooden finger thing
Shoulderblades frayed the cloth I'm made of
Sewn up my neck round speaking hole
and ragged with snot
pale salmon concealer sodden
I pick and pick the seam all day
does I really think anything covers me up
this my swan is it
eyes at one end cunt at the other
a swaying hurting wonder between
which is posture perfect

More glamorough
more pretooty

This is the way to the hall with the priest-holes Cathy

2 SECTIONS FROM "IMITATING"

I soaped myself & presented

myself in a   soft light

a breathing light
~~I would thank you~~
    for embracing me
& your head, then I was pushing away on your head with my feet
                into a huge bright horse I was inside of,

& I knew I was imitating, because my legs could make no gestures
that had not already been made. Why was I writing so much?
Because I was impressed, & saddled up & ridden.

M y greed was outrageous
power-outageous

       I felt all better & feverish
my braincase was
     hypertranslucent
& exercised with rumpling
tumbling skin
which I held gently
  over my brain
like a blanket
  or a weird threat
of cutting it off
from the world.
Oh my god. My
chest got cut off in
the mine.
I was mine & I was going
to dig myself a jewel.
I dug a little bone in me
I dug a little boneshaped
hole in me, I loved it
Hello you fuckers!
Dug around in there making
    my emergencies go off
I thought they were lovebells
  or runaway truck ramps

I'm hungry.

ALL BAR ONE

nigh said I made that up to
get some sweeteye from you all
some glance at me even if my
story is boring and a lie
nigh am so sick of doubting
myself an thinking I am bad
nigh bore myself
anyway trying to be like the udders
and who fuckin cares they don't
want me to be likem and borem
everybody dead.
Since I been here SCARED
and my natural EBULLISHNESS
held back by a warning finger.
Mo lady! Poop it out!
They lovit run yawling
scared and come back for more.
My natural LOVE tucked into
DESIRE I am folded into
envelope just hoping to
receive some love from the
eyes bent away bent
now but Unfold the flaps
and be a Page girl to the World

THE ARGUMENT

This book is called Hypneratomachia Fuckphila.
Fuckfila on her journey her new spelling
reminiscent of Chick-Fil-A. Fill the
chick and filler well of ding ding dong.
Fuckin' A. Behold a useful and
profitable book. If you think otherwise,
do not lay the blame on the book, but on
yourself. If you sourly refuse
the new erotic guest, do not despise
the well-ordered sequence nor the fine
well-ordered style. Then in this volume
she falls in love. It is a worthy book, and full
of many ornaments: he who will not read it
is dull of mind. Various things are treated in it
which it would tire me to relate, but accept
the work which offers a cornucopia
emending it should it be incorrect. The End.

FOR THE BOYS

Can you imagine dear men
what it is to be a woman being fucked.
The men installing a new gate
– ran past them prickling, face
prickling, back of neck
  sensitive and tight, and they do
say something to/about me

                    Now there was

in a transparent skybox
someone watching my body and giving it
a score.   I berated myself for letting it
hover; then the man in the orange construction helmet
 crashed through the skybox glass
with his head,
and the transparent box
filled with color and a stone support
under it. I did not make it up.

Will you just fuck me or
will I just fuck without the skybox.
There is no fucking without the skybox.

This part is for girls, college highschool girls

The guy fucks you five eight minutes
you think you are supposed to come

you do not. What's wrong with you?
frigidaire girl.
 "—But prior girl came all the time!"
To have to learn to be pleasing
throws his image
 as successful lover

—image he needs, to continue sexing—

  in doubt.

The problem lies
with you.

This situation   lie on both sides

is the rule. There are exceptions.

Now let us have ceremonial
sex.

Who is the pauper?

I will be.   I will be.

from WHITE MAN POEMS

My lover is a white man
Who else
My daddy
Who else.
The president is going to be impeached.
Some white men let me tell them what to do.
I said to one cut half these poems out your manuscript.
He is so grateful!
Wait for the white man to pick me up either in a station wagon or a blue van.
White man half an hour late!
I have been faithful to you white-man-area in my fashion. Ernest Dowson
That sounds like an early-twentieth-century black man but it is a nineteenth century
white man.
Smell of an old sock
His anus smell like an old dollar bill
But you can't just have a little something on the side

You have to feel sorry for them
You have to feel sorry for them

But I am, I am one.
They don't know that.
They let me drive their car,
If I was President,
NONSTOP LICKY
I'm afraid I can't think without licky
White man wrote almost every book in that shelf
Some nice guys
I sit with them, make healthy sonnet-juice
What are Jews are they all the way white?
The Jews spring to mind

Am not required to praise, required to love I am

Praise for him falls short of what himself can give

I ask a lot, and so I do receive from him

I ask nothing, and nothing do I gain of him
                          He asks nothing

Lie down now in cold blanket having bitchy thoughts
Aggression will out here or it will out elsewhere
He knows he's meant to keep the phone away from me
(My sister, come to town, she doesn't trust me much)

Sounds like he's going to keep the phone away from me

Must write poems to fill the huge demand for them

MACULAR HOLE

Please god love me and buy me

Read this hillock and ride me
Wraith typing all day for money.

God bought me today for two silver fish in a can
God bought me tomorrow for bland in a pan
and a card an email from Rebecca

Bought four hours of my control alt delete shut down
Bought a new day-section with a headstand

My commerce in shall

Sky like a grandstand
Transact

God performed me today for a half minute
lucky
in locker room hiding my boobs from the kids
and my hair is silky and my mane shot silk gold

Bought a book on economy
Georgie Bataille
Called about plane tickets
Georgie Bataille
I bought my debt today
Georgie Bataille hooray
Debt off my God today

God off my debt in a macular hole

I dream of an end like a fount to this night
Run thinner and thinner and then it's all light
Macerated in signal

by my go

I bought my ghost I walk my ghost

CATHY PARK HONG

ALMANAC

Blood tone   flood tone
woods over-swarmed with description
starless   riotous   woods

writhing nor with wolf nor lion.
Writhed with guides who emerged
with their chromatic lore

paved arteries   hotels   grease-shined
with locals   we guide   guide
I am crammed with tongues   crammed

with guides who ache for their own
guides   who mourn   who lead
men from human rinds of discontent,

shuttle mutiny   *stench and swelter*
aborigine who leads vested men through
stream snake   brush   who gust

shave your hair ulcerate your nemesis
guide to spectral love   to animal behavior
to coitus in a hot tub

a cherry tour bus skidded   overturned
travelers shimmied out in droves while
inflammable gases blushed out

fish lens porn   bushel of mustard spices
2nd world auto dealers   rotisserie roar
of champagne volcanoes

I paddle down the bodies with an oar's
thwack   the storage of migrants kept
under   gouting   stream

Is that gun fire? Rat-a-tat?
What cadaverous blooms?   Face smear
against my windshield   crying

we will tar you with birds
succor soon   yassir   a fleet of skiffs
zigzag paths   look here to sylvan arroyo

flattened tonsil   woods break off
into series   coma
oh radiant lives

all guides
all beautiful   erroneous
unison.

2. THE HULA HOOPER'S TAUNT
(*from* MUSIC OF THE STREETS SERIES)

I'mma two-ton spiker   hips fast rondeau
n'ere more nay sayer   feel this orbit rattle

Wipe that that prattle   that spittle   crass pupa
gupta   away you   ma' man,

where you   revolving   solving
spin shorty   shark   satellitic   fever

Leer not, lyre   I spiral atom pattern
faster than you say my turn.

Note from the Historian
We wandered into a stadium where thirteen hundred people competed for the national hula hoop-
er's contest. The last one standing won the contest. While hula-hooping, they taunted their neigh-
bors to discourage them. From your seats, you could not actually hear them but I snuck onto the
grounds where I overheard the invective. I also enjoyed sitting high up on the bleachers to listen
to the deafening rattle of thirteen hundred hula hoops in action.

KARAOKE LOUNGE

Impish peeper, impish peeper, you ear-dropping?
When I ululate til mine fes a grapey pulp,
croaking K-pop en dis privacy-room? Me bumming,
see? Shoo, ga, tour is ova, scug...
Shoo...

Non. . . no, stay. Stay,
Some sing swallow nightingales. *Ahem*...
phlegm, some sing swallow nightingale en agora,
but we closet singas en a box,

a mike—a grog sodden salary man sing, "0 lore,
no harem, jus' mefelf," he keens, til he lurch
into him mike wit no invocatory might, him lung
raisined like him balls, he sleepim, dreaming o
tong-il o *tigers in red weather*...

We sing solo, tone-deaf,
gargle a bauble, it pops dead o night...
Anon, Sinatra canon...Aska ballad bloom
en room din buzza stop,
So ye want to hear me story? Ab initio?
'Bout mine domus, 'bout Sah?

Mine madder, rest her soul, sang fo all,
lung a fireplace breatha, bronchial tree aflarne til she spit
a blood wad, she sang pansori, one beat
drum a ko bell. Whole day a story sung, tong-seung!

Aiiiree...Airreee...epic song lasting
twotreefo day...sponge up de Han...ssulp'un yaegge...
Ssarang-han nam'pyun...wit only a fan y jug to wet her troat...

ZOO

Ga   The fishy consonant,
Na   The monkey vowel.

Da   The immigrant's tongue
       as shrill or guttural.

Overture of my voice like the flash of bats.
The hyena babble and apish libretto.

Piscine skin, unblinking eyes.
Sideshow invites foreigner with the animal hide.

Alveolar *tt*, sibilant *ss*, and glottal *hh*

shi:	poem
kkatchi :	magpie
ayi:	child

Words with an atavistic tail. History's thorax considerably
cracked. The Hottentot click called undeveloped.

Mother and Father obsessed with hygiene:
as if to rid themselves of their old third world smell.

Labial *bs* and palatal *ts*:

La   the word
Ma   speaks
Ba   without you

I dreamed a Korean verse, a past conversation
with Mother when they said I was blathering unintelligibly
in my sleep.

The mute girl with the baboon's face unlearned
her vowels and cycled across a rugged phonetic map.

Sa	glossary
Au	din
Ja	impossible word

Macaws turned into camouflaged moths.
The sky was overcast, the ocean a slate gray

along the wolf-hued sand. I dived into the ocean
swam across channels to islands without flags;

replaced the jingoist's linotype with my yellowing
canines and shrilled against the anemic angel who

cradled the bells that dictated time and lucid breath.

ALL THE APHRODISIACS

blowfish arranged on a saucer. Russian roulette. angelic slivers.

ginseng, cut antlers allotted in bags dogs on a spit, a Dutch girl

winking holds a bowl of shellfish.

white cloth, drunkenness. a different language leaks out—
the idea of throat, an orifice, a cord—

you say it turns you on when I speak Korean.

The gold paste of afterbirth, no red—

Household phrases   *—pae-go-p'a*   (I am hungry)
                               —ch'i-wa   (Clean up)
                               —kae sekki   (Son of a dog)

I breathe those words in your ear, which make you climax;

afterwards you ask me for their translations. I tell you it's a secret.

gijek niin tigit rril—the recitation of the alphabet; guttural diphthong, gorgeous.

What are the objects that turn me on: words—

han-gul: the language first used by female entertainers, poets, prostitutes.

The sight of shoes around telephone wires, pulleyed by their laces, the blunt
word cock.

Little pink tutus in FAO Schwarz,
when I was four they used to dress me as a boy,

white noise, whitwashed. the whir of ventilation in the library.

Even quarantined amongst books, I tried to kiss you once.

Strips of white cotton, the color of the commoner, the color of virtue,
the color that can be sullied—

my hand pressed against your diaphragm, corralling your pitch,

a pinch of rain caught between mouths,

analgesic, tea. poachers drawing blood—

strips of white cotton I use to bind your wrist to post, tight
enough to swell vein, allow sweat—

sweat to sully the white of your sibilant body,

the shrug of my tongue, the shrug of command, *sssshhht.*

RITE OF PASSAGE

Childhood was spent in an open dressing room where
white women pulled chenille over their breasts and

I felt oddly collaged: elbow to nose, shin to eye,
neck to breast, brow to toe

When I flirted, marbles slivered out of my mouth
like amphibious eggs.

Hey saekshi, the American GIs cried to the Korean
barmaids, pronouncing *saekshi* 'sexy'

though *saekshi* meant respectable woman,
a woman eligible for marriage.

The arterial clouds shouldered a glassy reservoir.
Divers made thin sleeves in the water,

Fog rolled over the dry shrub mountains
like air conditioning.

She's back, the saleslady whispered to her assistant,
when Mother came to try on a blouse.

A rain of Rapunzels fell from their towers,
bodies first, hair trailing like streamers.

My first kiss was with a twenty-year-old man
who whispered *your hands are shaking*.

When thoughts of disgrace invaded the mind,
I hummed or sang to drown out the noise.

A stutter inflated and reddened the face:
eyes bulged and lips gaped to form,

a fortune cookie creaked and a tongue rolled out.
Wagged the Morse code but no one knew it.

Antidepressants lined up like clever pilgrims.
I felt quiet that night.

Fragments of freaks: the Hottentot's ass,
the Siamese twins' toupee, the indecisive chink

who said, I do. Later, no forget it, I do not.

ON SPLITTING

Wind does not whip, it caresses. Or it whips when a mail order song crescendos in the background. The blowsy sails. The fat, fat sky.

We blow air bubbles. Once they touch the dry outer skin of your lips, they pop: a pocket of unsaid gas.

The taste of body, the drumming on lard. A kind of love that has become autistic.

Mother and Father on the hilt of a sugary cake. An avalanche but a minor one that tastes of confectionery. Photographs of Mother the bride. A stiff smile that does not like dairy.

Denote passion.

A Korean wedding. There is a sign for blushing: two perfect red circles pasted on the bride's cheeks. Or it's a sign for passion, good luck, or maybe it's to hide the pallor.

The girl takes the knife, the boy takes from her, the girl takes the knife, the boy takes it from her, the girl takes the knife, the boy takes it from her, the girl takes the knife, the boy takes it from her.

The stage is set for the woman with the killer whale eyes. She announces, "there is no love, only longing."

My mother said, "If you eat lying down, you'll grow hair on your crotch."

To find passion, I should have written a lyric poem. A poem that would roll off the tongue like icing, curdles curds, whey, icing, a cube of ice.

The first Korean man I liked shared a plate of squid with me. I called him brother because I was much younger than he. Chewing on a flank, he told me he'd slept with five women and fallen in love with one.

I grew a petri dish of princes, all replicating and jostling each other for my hand.

Afterwards, we kissed in the dark enclaves of a stuffy TV room. Our tongues were not sure of each other and our breaths stank of salted squid. It was not what I fantasized.

I am here to lick your shoes, your hairy shins, your eventual cock.

My parents never kissed in public. Except once. An obligaton on the cheek before my father left.

The word most often said during lovemaking: *ttagawu*. This could mean itchy or spicy. The same word used when wearing a wool sweater that irritates, or easing into a tub of scalding water.

I would have preferred a sealed letter, even a terse message taped to the refrigerator. Rather than the talk, the awkwardness of it, the restraint. *A letter daggers her heart*—dagger. The histrionics of dagger.

To restrain.

Adolescent obsessions: Greek mythology, heavy metal rock stars, documentation of freaks (Mexican midget, triplets, albino sword swallowers), iron-on T-shirts, breasts, he who gave you your first bong hit and kiss.

Along the soldered road, he lies motionless. I arrive and crouch down. Kiss his rigor mortis lips and he rises. This is a holy scripture or a movie.

We barely knew each other yet he confessed to me until his face clattered off like a hubcap.

Restraint turns passion into shame. Or worse, martyrs. My mother comes from a country of martyrs, a fetish of martyrs, a crateful of martyrs.

This is not a precious jade bracelet. It is plastic, given to me by my Italian friend who bought it for 50 cents.

The girl takes the knife.

I don't know the Korean word for sex. I ask Mother. Father, a couple of aunts. What's the word? They feign ignorance. I ask a friend living in Seoul. Even she doesn't know. "There are many words that refer to it. Just not one definite one."

Along the soldered road, there is a man sleeping. I pause, wanting to kiss him. But I am apprehensive that he would awake, become offended or confused. I shut the book, earmark the page, shut the book.

CHELSEY MINNIS

PREFACE 1

People say "nothing new" or "the death of the author" but, I am new and I am not dead.

Intellectual, anachronistic, superserious: I'm not going to start crying because "experimental" and I'm not going to start crying because "not experimental"...I just want to piss down my own leg...

And should everyone be bored like narcosis?....

Poetry should be "uh huh" like..."baby has to have it..."

If anyone thinks they need to write reviews, teach classes, edit magazines or translate books in order to write good poetry...then maybe they should just take a rest from it...

If you try to write a good poem again and again for years and years and receive no awards, no money, no nothing ....then you're happy...

And all these blurbs are for s---. Like if I were to carry around a turd and pretend it is my baby...

The poet I worship is Edward Dorn, because I adore his disgust...

Whatever he says feels like art...

Poetry is for crap since there's no money or fast cars in it...

But, in the thighs...I feel it...

PREFACE 13

When I write a poem it's like looking through a knothole into a velvet fuckpad...

And it is like buttery sweetbreads spilled down the front of your dress...

It is like a gun held to the head of a poodle...

If I want to write any poems I will write them!

A poem that doesn't have any intellectual filler in it...

Like two blondes fighting on a roof...

PRIMROSE

...............when my mother..

....was raped..

....

....a harpsichord began to play...........................

....red candles melted.....and...........................

.............spilled down the mantle...

....there was blood in the courtyard......

.............................and blood on the birdbath..

.......and blood drizzled.....on brown flagstones...

....as a red fox bared its teeth...............................

.....................white harts...................froze...

..........and snow hares fled...and left.............

....heartshaped footprints in the snow.....................

....that melted..............

....

..........in the spring when I was born...

....

....

....

..............and it is torture......for my mother.......................that I am now luscious

....and she is dead.

....

....

...........and that I have..

..............................bare shoulders..

....and a flower behind my ear.......................

....

....

..........as I beat gentleman rapists...

....

....................with bronze statuettes...

..........so that the blood...................oozes down their handsome sideburns............

....or give them..........................

..........a poisoned mushroom..

....

....or corsages and corsages of gunshot

FIFI, NO, NO

"Fifi, I thought I told you to stop touching me with your soft little hands....."

Fifi: "The weakness of Fifi..."

"Fifi, it is not possible for you to continue behaving in this manner..."

I am fallen in love with by a young girl: Fifi.

Fifi			
takes hand	strokes hair	sits too close	puts hand on knee

1. Fifi should not touch my breast with her hand...

It is very very depressing when Fifi falls on her face on the flagstones and doesn't cry.

We don't like to hold each other's hands and dance with sparklers!

"She is a girl but she is Fifi."

Fifi again
- touching with hands
- holding face still to try to kiss it
- whispering
- petting hair with delight

Fifi, go away with your sparklers, I am not for you...

"Fifi at night!... Fifi at night!..."

Fifi: eating a hamburger...

Fifi, infidel of nothing

Fifi of the iron will of caressing

No acceptance of refusals, no allowances, no resistance, no taking away of the hand, no.

All this foretelling a bad end: Fifi to be completely patronized and tolerated by everybody which is a disgrace...

UH

..uh.....................I want to wear hot pants..

....

....and rest my boot on the back

of a man's neck...

....

....and..........

....take a sharp cane..................

.....................and....................stick my heart....................like...a piece of trash

...............in a park..

.....................and...

....

....

rise out of arctic waters with curled icicles in my hair and a speargun...................

....

....and..

............buy a lazy game cat with claws.................that scratch me......................

....and..........................uh!................

....

....

....

...............someone should knock me down.. and press me against blue tile...........

....and shuck........................

a gold sheath dress............................off me.....................................

....and push...

........a shiny buzzer...

.......................to make me slide down a glistening chute...

....

....because......................I am sique.....

....

....

.............................of everyone and opposed to everyone................and just want

....total emasculation...

....so I can...

....pluck the grey beards of old men..

....

...................................and...

....give them....

............hairline fractures..

............and a row of forest green stitches.......................above their right eyes.....

....

......or then just...

.......................bleed in a sailor suit..........................and salute them and faint........

....

....so...............................they can bang

my mouth against a balcony railing..or.....................

....cut my head off...

....

....because I am too.............................petulant..........

....

....

....

....and..............................I.......want them to..

....centre death blows between..............

....my shoulder blades...and...............then.....

....gently lick electrodes.......and stick

them to my temples...

....

...................because...

....

........................I must...

....

....take a silken pull cord...........................

and pull......it...

...................and fall through a trapdoor.........................and...................

..................escape on a chrome war sleigh drawn by arctic huskies...........and........

....uh...................

....................someone should........................come towards me...................

.............frowning with a knife...

....

...........................and butterfly my flesh...

....

..................and..try to...................................

........................give me...

....oral....................maxillofacial kisses...............

....

.........and then hit me with a brickbat...

....

.......and shoot me..........with round plump bullets...............while I'm lounging....

.............with a leopard pillow...

.......................because.....................................uh...

....

....otherwise.............................

...........tears slide out from under my cateye sunglasses......................

TIGER D

I am a tiger or a daughter or both...

Of course I am a tiger and a daughter but I am a show tiger...everyone demands it because of my deep fur...

I like to fall in love with my trainers....

There is a desire to touch tigers and there is a desire to hold them, so I am not entirely lost...

I am meant to parade my fur and growl. In addition I am a good show daughter but only for show...

I don't like my servitude as a tiger...but I like baby bottles of cream....

As I daughter I am ferocious, but as a tiger I must be pleasing...which is impossible...as I do not wish it...

As a daughter I am horrid which is my wish..

She-tigers can be dangerous and drowsy which means they are content...

As a tiger I'm more drugged and more soft in the fur and therefore more valuable to the blind...

As I am a daughter I can be amused, but as a tiger I cannot be amused or I will turn murderess...

But if I am a tiger and a daughter then I better be good...

I better reform myself to receive practical instruction and not be a slut-o

It is bad to be a daughter but worse to be a tiger.

SECTIONAL

Then you are terrible and striped....

.......I sink into a reverie in leather......................sectional couches.....................

.................with caramel in my mouth...

....so that I am reliving......................................

....a moment and revolving..................

.................caramel as I am surrounded on all sides by.....................................

.......................soft panels of genuine...

....

.......................leather.......and I run my hand along the leather unknowingly.......

....

...........as I oralize the caramel and soften it as I am..

....

....loosening and loosening..........

.....................into my dreaminess.....with a faroff composure......................and...

....

.............................launching my molars...................into the cluster..................

in order to.....locate...

.............the nucleus..

.......................of the caramel with my mouth and.......maul the unformed mass...

.......................with my tongue..

.............and really lounge..

.......................in the passive leather...

......sectional...couch...with 12 separable sections..alone.....................................

....

....

....as I try to evaluate.....................the reverie............

.................in the enormous moments...

on the couch made of soft skins...that are compressed...

....

..................................as I chew the mutable caramels.....................................

....and clench..............

my jaw..and demolish them...........................

...........................in the durable moments...

....

........................with a soft formation in my mouth..........and the memories..............

....that are unavoidable.......................

....

................and the pliable anger........towards myself...

................for lazing on tender leather...

.................................and hauling up the...............delicate past.................

....

....on the casual...........................

....

........modular couch with padded armrests..

....where I can rest my arms

WENCH

..as I revisit sorrowful..and frightening moments...of happiness that must have occurred..

I want to get straight through life like➤-➤-➤-➤-➤-➤-➤-➤-➤-➤-➤-➤-➤-➤-➤-➤-➤-➤-➤

Sometimes I have to throw up and pass out in order to get to the next set of time increments. Because otherwise time forms into a hard migraine like a gumball.

I want to wear fluted sleeves and become like a darling person with appropriateness all around me...

If I am proactive I can really attempt to be a good person with waterfalls behind me and a bird on my wrist.

Sometimes I want to tear laundry off of laundry lines. Or swim out to a floating platform to kiss someone.

I should be thought of as a fiend. But I am a strumpet or an abyss. Like a groove, like azure. I am a wench like azure. This is what a girl thinks when she is jumping rope.

It is rough to be a seafoam wench. like cocksucker. Like kissing someone and then spitting into their mouth.

Oval like a wench. Like the tusk of a moth. But with a club in my hand. Like freshly drilled stargazer holes...

I know some thing. It keeps coming to me when I wake up. A pang like a black band around my head.

I am a wench at night and that means I sink into it like an overstuffed chair.

How can you be so mild when I am ready to hit? Because I'm sorry like a clavier I really am. I'm sorry like a milktruck.

I have to get down to the ground. When everyone is gliding on conversations. I am panting inside like a cub.

At night, I reach out to my drinks....

DANIELLE PAFUNDA

MY SEA LEGS

From then on, Zorba called me "Princess of Quite-a-Lot."
She said my body became a praise-shack. From the catalogue,
a new bed. From the neighbor's bed, a lace wig. She stenciled
the ripe pets herself. She upholstered my vanity table in shag.

She took aside her little nephew and for fun they mapped a city.
In the pocket, she had charcoals, pastels, crayons, ochres. Rot.
He drew a drawbridge, she drew a gangplank. He an awning,
she an armory. In the city hall, a buck hung. Black lung.
Gallows. They drew a dock for me, a to and fro for bad days,
and wrought a trip-trap iron caisson with the top down.

A QUARTER-HOUR OF RECESS

In the schoolyard, Zorba wanted to compare genies.
With another girl. A panty-waist. He called me Russian.
The Russians are coming. A broken strand of panties.
Wind. Then, profile, he coaxed a match from the placket.

A set of stumps at various heights, rendered the red, blue,
yellow of the time. We ventured an alligator, a predation,
irked by little feet as the troll was. Irked by gruff not gruff
enough. The permanent shiver. We rode it.

He took turns on me. We performed a dance known as
"under doggies," and when that was banned, we called it
"under over." In the present tense, the school demanded.
I, you, we, they forgive. He and she forgives.

SALON

A funnel. A truly great endeavor; enclosure. Here,
a whiskey handshake in a metal glove. A turnstile
for lovers. The sardine can wears like a rosebud,
we call the cloister generous, we service the unbearable
cliquing of cliché. Dramamine.

A suitor. At the doctor's. We talked about the lovely
Herculine, as if we weren't ourselves girls about to find out
that we were actually boys finding out that we were still
a little bit girl. Infernally. We weren't ourselves the governess,
dreaming herself the renegade, tied to the tracks, untying herself
from the tracks, riding to safety, frothing as the horse does.

And the doctor conducted a series of x-rays.

A parlor game.

You can read one's fortune

by counting the blockage.

FABLE

When he was mine, I'd milk him. Make his hair
grow. He was, at first, a liar. He was actually
employed by the circus. He was a fandango.
A woman with a nine-foot penis. An inch.

The ghosts of two wives met him at the foot
of the bed. The first with resin-coated hairpiece
and second with red nail lacquer. No. He was
only afraid of the little wolves who lived behind
the little wool skirts. Of girls in closets.

I pooled his underwear around my own ankles.
The cordite hairs on his back sang a chorus. I took.
His pockets, complicit. I gave, too. A plump.
My lithesome peacock, fanned tail feathers. The cinder.

WHO CHOSE ELIZABETH SIDDAL

I was that world's exotic prison rat. My cuffs mule-feathered,
my tail pump and plump. I was allowed one rubber spoon,
and a box of tapioca seed. Each sunrise, I traced the perimeter,
searching out hotspots, mixing a fat pot of paste. For a time,
I knew that carrot to be spun gold and imminent.

Then I knew. Immanent. What stupid riddles strung, eyelash
and false, a slew of rhinestone tears—their prongs, my puss.

And though I could wiggle between bars, flip the light switch,
the cafeteria and laundry, mine, steaming, deserted, I couldn't
skip beyond its reckless walls. It was red shoes and pixie dust
from there to the crypt. So when the tongue-twister came for me,

I opened wide and wider went.

 The fuckwad says, my dear, my doughy dewy doe-eyed dimple,
you mustn't attempt to think while you Sphinx. You
mustn't leave the room now, for you haven't ever yet.
And what will Odd Job think? What will he odious
pus in the empty nest with a piddle of wire and a prong?
What will he when he gets in your grille and finds
that you've gone?

> Advice will be heeded even as you attempt to head

Look you after that corset, which strings trick you out
and whip you floss again. Look you above, a halo
to still your roving mag eye. Taken won't you? With
his obliging fig paw? His homoeothermic enterprise?

The fuckwad says, really, a number of wolves?
Think you not actually mice in the glut? Oughtn't you ignore
mice, foul weather, other shod feet shambling? Whatever

I AM NOW YOUR OWN PRIVATE SPOOK BRIGADE

the world, it hasn't called. It hasn't lifted your lip.
Check me, fun wig candy spun ringlet red to ultra,
a peignoir smocked breast tattered ladder stitch ribbon
greased up hem, reflective glasses from the chop cop.
Nothing, though, 'til you see my stickware.

Dinner's under the sheet. Squirmy, fixed yet. A ring
of salt, charred some, table's edge. I'll have you know
it's a stew.

A grim little sliver that fits the ignition, a grape scented
fibrous gallon of puncture. A tutelage ripe in fringe
sanitation, don't you tell me I never you nothing you did.

The fuckwad wants to compare nonfeelings. Wick
stumper cesspool torquing slack bastion cracks wide.
I hoof it through Ugly Park to the fixit. A salve please,
an antibacterial spill theorem. Freak tag my chart please,
my lick please, my rigged stop heart thwack. Slushing.

A swab please.
insidethe gates
perched. Chairs
peace farce. Oh pill
zone

**Whichever pen you use
to sign, your own blood
issues**

Outside the crow birds on gates and
close, the astrologers fluffed and ready,
banal, savannah ink blot stone fed Z
me. Still me stinking ripe face gone

proof.

Slow me and fence it. I hock shop I gold play I leaking
valuables. There is a window, roll call, a vile plastic stack.

HORSE

The womb, a tick-tock, a shrapnel bearing croc. Daylight scum
rigging, turpentine swilling. Next the cog, glutted on tubal despair,
freak-white on the far side of her bone-bright cell. Shorn
as her familiar.

Lip, carnelian bitch-froth. Airless hiss, worn in a scythe. Skin glove
laced tight, a wax doll mildewed sinking limb. Great hole
full of mouth-holes. Eye-holes, cavities and sugar cubes.

The hog box hums beneath fetid petticoat.
Cats have been among the beds.

Spoon up the fatty stars from their reeking swarming broth. Pin
the siren through her thorny pap. A figurehead for your toxic rick.
Claim her fussing milk-stained bairns, little men, precious
in their dampened fleece.

A stainless gothic quill stakes each retina in its rubber globe.
A Death's brow pearl for every last admirer, for every winsome brute.

GURLESQUE: THE VISUAL ARTS

The sculpture, graffiti, painting, embroidery, and installation pieces in these pages represent acts of disobedience to our collective fictions about what it means to be female. As with their poet counterparts, Gurlesque visual artists co-opt a damaging history of sexist slurs and gross misrepresentations of girls and women and turn it on its head, making facile stereotypes creak at the hinges, complicating their signification through defiant overanimation. Their highly visceral work draws on such predecessors as Hannah Hoch's Dada collages, Frida Khalo's paintings, Cindy Sherman's photographs and Marina Abramovic's and Karen Finley's performance art. With edgy, bombastic humor, Gurlesque artists unceremoniously reject social norms and invite us to re-imagine the uses of our bodies and our desires.

A bit about the artists and images in this portfolio:

Lauren Kalman creates unconventional objects of female adornment that resemble malignant excrescences or cancerous growths, playing with received notions of material worth and beauty. Lady Aiko, who first gained notoriety from her participation in the legendary Street Art collective Faile, creates bold works of art that mix Japanese pop-culture and classic Western pinup-style icons with a distinctive Street Art-informed aesthetic. In her cut-paper silhouettes, Kara Walker draws on images from the antebellum South, slave narratives, and minstrel shows, conflating fact and fiction to reveal the still-shocking roots of racial and gender bias. Hope Atherton's sculpture and painting invoke the 18th century curio cabinet gone luridly and magnificently awry. She manipulates found objects such as animal skins and rusted pieces of metal to construct sculptural fantasias that include the mummified corpses of unicorns and long-clawed monsters. Dame Darcy's deliciously wicked comic series, *Meat Cake*, and the Goth-vaudevillian silent films, handmade dolls, and jug bands that accompany it, are populated by an uncanny cast of characters drawn from freak and sideshows, fairytales, bluegrass ballads and other morbid flotsam of Americana. Alessandra Exposito constructs a trophy wall made from the flamboyantly decorated skulls of beloved pets. The meticulous detailing lavished on each skull evokes the intimacy of a private fetish object, and combines a rhinestone-encrusted flavor with traditional Mexican-American memorial art. Audrey Kawasaki's precise technical style reveals the dual influences of manga comics and Art

Nouveau; a number of her soft-core, melancholy waifs are eerily accessorized with chicken bones, tentacled sea creatures, or their own throbbing organs. E.V. Day, who often works in large-scale installation, is represented here by assemblages of clamshells, animal tongues, liquid that simulates menstrual blood and other grotesque detritus, "reconstructing" disembodied female organs that wink and menace.

The work of these nine women testifies to the fact that, as in the poetry world, Gurlesque visual art is alive and kicking. It's not only kicking: it's a widespread phenomenon that surfaces in a variety of ways across the contemporary scene. (Given enough time and money, we'd put together a CD of Gurlesque music, too. Maybe someday soon.) And the artists selected here are representative, but not alone: the Gurlesque is present in the work of many other younger women artists in painting, installation, video and other genres. Taken collectively, Gurlesque visual artists are, to use the words of Björk (that hyper-Gurlesque songstress), "Smooth soft red velvety lungs / pushing a network of oxygen joyfully." We are invigorated by their work, and so glad to be able to present them alongside their literary kin.

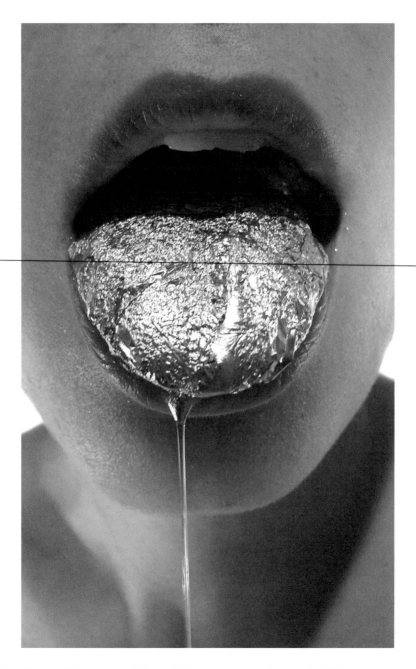

Hard Wear (Tongue Gilding), Lauren Kalman, Digital print, laminated on acrylic, 2006

St. Kitty, Lady Aiko, Mixed media on paper, 2007

Lady Kill, Lady Aiko, Mixed media on paper, 2008

Endless Conundrum, An African Anonymous Adventuress, Kara Walker, Paper, 2001

Authenticating the Artifact, Kara Walker, Cut paper and acrylic on gessoed panel, 2007

Starfish, Hope Atherton, Mixed media, 1998

Virgin Taming, Hope Atherton, Suri alpaca wool, mixed rock putty, suede, felt, hot glue, 2002

"Nails" from *Meat Cake #16*, Dame Darcy, Pen and ink, 2007

"Picture Perfect" from *Meat Cake #16*, Dame Darcy, Pen and ink, 2007

Lulabelle, Alessandra Exposito, Mixed media on cat skull, 2007

Gigi, Alessandra Exposito, Mixed media on chicken skull, 2006

Hakuchou no Shi, Audrey Kawasaki, Oil and graphite on wood, 2008

My Dishonest Heart, Audrey Kawasaki, Mixed media on wood, 2008

Pearl Diver, E. V. Day, Coyote tongues, freshwater pearls, thong, glass, resin, 2004

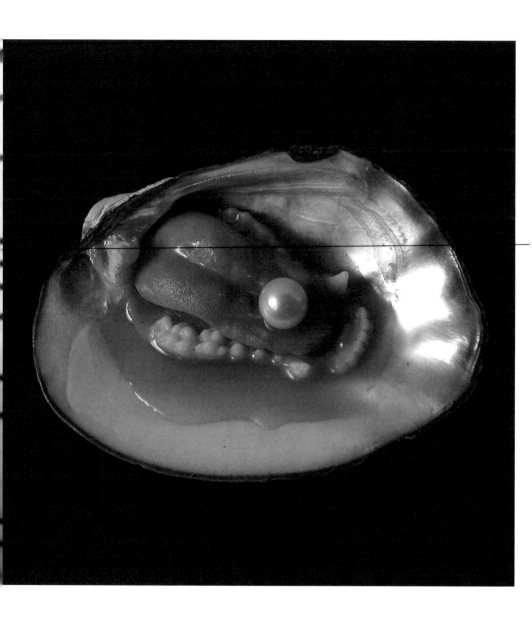

Abalone, Raccoon Jaw and Tongue with Mother of Pearl and Resin, E. V. Day, 2005

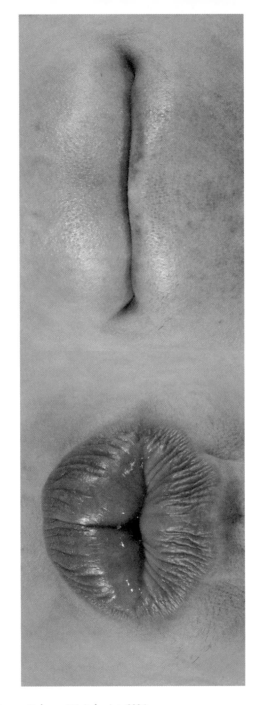

Pursed and Puckered, Lauren Kalman, Digital print, 2006

DOROTHEA LASKY

BOOBS ARE REAL

They stole my tires
They knocked down my house
They killed my father
They cut off my fingers
And I thought, "And I did like those fingers."

They pierced my eyelids. They scalped my brain.
They ran their sweaty fingers down my sweaty back.
They played me music but it wasn't music.
They loved me and then they didn't.
Somewhere in there I grew these enormous boobs.
At some point what they took away
Was given back
In the form of boobs.
What they took from me
They gave back
Just like, as Lydia Davis says,
When a limit has been reached
What is real but does not help
Is lost forever and replaced by the unreal.
The difference is: these boobs are real.

TEN LIVES IN MENTAL ILLNESS

Anorexia

A bird is flying above a forest. I could say he was a blackhawk but what's the difference? There is nothing living in the forest. Except the trees are there and the mudwort, but nothing is living like the bird. The bird is flying above the forest. One wing is bent. He is trying to make sense of the hole in his chest. *Holey Moley* he says spinning around the forest, and the trees and the wuddleflowers spin around, *Holey Moley* they say and laugh with him.

Mania

I am in a blue sea and I am wearing a red nightie. The nightie has been ripped in places most of all by the nighttime. This sea is made of girdledoves and thing-a-ma-bobs. O yes and Bob too. Bob is kissing me and giving me flowers. He is giving me 8 headaches with his spinning finger. The finger he has made to court me but he does not realize no man who lives shall court me or please me. It is God who pleases me with his high and mighty and his amen and the room stretched out in light like a thin muscle flayed into the sun.

Insomnia

The young thing wrapped the fruit in sequins and showed it to the nun. The nun said good day and got it a goldfish. She got it a goldfish and special gloves to handle herself and the fish. The night is always full of surprises, I tell them now. The moonflowers had been dyed black in hell and the nun and the thing knew it. They both knew the thing would one day murder the nun, its thick fingers coiling and wrapping tightly around the nun's neck.

Depression

The stars are made of yellow paper but I did not know this for a long time so I wandered a marshy place looking for The Green Leprechaun. The Leprechaun and I were good friends even though he was a Capricorn and wore strangely pungent gloves. We ate dinner together on Tuesdays and Wednesdays and after dinner I'd curl his hair and give him lemon drops. I'd slide the drops down his big throat like good old Aunt Lolly used to do to me and give him a bath in Kaluha.

Obsessive Compulsive Disorder

The murder took place on a day that was made for the children. He took the children and mashed them into a bucket. He made us eat it. I had to eat it! Afterwards he smelled his fingers so we smelled our fingers. Our hands stunk but actually quite sweetly. We all wore matching socks that were green and tan. The green was a nice green like the green an apple makes in the summer heat.

Paranoia

I fell in love once with a train conductor. He used to oil the trains with his urine and belch on himself. We would go places with his parents and they would belch too. No I wasn't surprised. My wits were always about me. I stayed demure like a demon, quietly reapplying my lipstick on the hour and half-hour. My lipstick was called Ancient Brick but really it was more of a mauve. Right before the love affair ended his mother and I would sneak in the bathroom together and change stockings.

Autism

A singer was trying to remember her songs but all she could think of was socks. *O Pasiphae, my Great Mother* she would cry *What has happened to my sight?* bumping around her tower like a blindball henchman. The tower stretched up forever into the heavens. 10 feet above her some crows perched and circled, then perched and circled. *Farewell* she sang and no one was listening.

Alzheimer's

I am made of lead, mushrooms, and rice. I am sitting here eating my blood (and yours too!) Come with me we will drink blood and brain! Come with me we will drink blood, brine, and brain! We are all children here made of folds and staples. We are made of folks that don't know we are listening. The ocean is floating above us like a quiet ring of moon. There is a ring of men here dancing around the moon throwing napkins at us.

Panic Attacks

In a dream I had a heart attack and forgot how to breathe. Then the dream followed me to my real life and no one would have sex with me. Not even the people I asked nicely. In the shower I would shake and shake. In the shower my husband would come in and try to have sex with me, but I did not want his dick. I wanted a row of dicks all filled to their tips with oxygen. I went from shower to bed, to shower to bed, never really getting anywhere.

Schizophrenia

A bunny came to my room and gave me a wish. He was actually part bunny and part man. He had waited for a new head but no one could find him one. His head was enormously large. He had walked into my room and smarted his head on the ceiling. *I am all head* I said and showed him I had no legs. He smiled and rubbed my tummy with a smooth washcloth and then a coarse one. There was nothing new in the world there at that moment and I assure you there is nothing new now either.

DIABETIC COMA

I got a brazilian wax for my engagement
But my old man was in a diabetic coma.
"Sweet Death!" he cried and I gave him a shove.
"Now this is the truth" we all thought
As he lay there, feeling nothing.
We pricked him and he whimpered a little,
But really nothing.
Four elusive spiders went crawling on him
But he had no human instinct
To grab at the elusivity.
I got my back-up dancers and we tempted
Him with the sin of women,
But his sugar level was so rich he couldn't see.
So we slipped him under the ground
And let the bugs eat him
Since that's what he really wanted anyway.

THE RED ROSE GIRLS

I.
The Red Rose Girls were unlikely girls
HD liked them anyway and they spent their time in the insides, growing soft.
Inside they were all mush, and roses rotting
And when people spoke to them their
Insides wilted from the inside
And not from the outside, which as it was,
Was bright and blue and plastic.

II.
There was a time the Red Rose Girls went into death
And death was untuned to them and he made them an unlikely hole
To hide themselves from anything
And the place they hid was mathematics and really was nothing
And also was its lesser art, astrology
Which of course is everything
And in math and astrology their heads burst out of the dragon
Like an unlikely pair
Of dragons, one with half a leg and
The other, untuned and slightly bumpy.

III.
The Red Rose Girls went out to
Sit on the beach and Woolf was there, her arms outstretched
And into them they went, she was their lost daughter
And kissing her arms extensively
She was bat-like and her arms outstretched
A great many oceans and they were all sisters, kissing the arms
Of a great eternity, too large to even be
Compared to things that are small.

And the picture they have of that day is on the dresser.
IV.
The Red Rose Girls told the day anything
For there is nothing the day
Can't handle, its bright smart being
The way hell out of war and marriage
They got their way out of war and marriage, those devilish leopards
Cancering and in them
The folds of the great bat,
Unlikely and mean.

V.
I am finally in The Red Rose Girls, and mean
I mean to say
I am in the girls and mean and can't get out
The place of me not mean and unstartled
And unlikely to be the rose all bunched up
In it its core is a universe of cats
And inside the universe is the scary sound of cats
Their heartbeats and hoofbeats making a universal mistake.

VI.
We the Red Rose Girls have made
A serious mistake, the universe is unlikely
Our hearts are sore, the roses
Our heads are folding over like the bat's, with wings outstretched
And in the brain is a wing
And unlikely that, a graph
Of Europe and the grizzly arts
Made by the machine men.
Their little metal hearts,
Elephant-like and supple.

THAT ONE WAS THE ODDEST ONE

That Robbie Wood is so weird
He seriously makes me want to fuck his brains out
Oh fuckable man, why do you have to do and say such
Strange things? Why if they were only all so weird
I would fuck them all night, their dicks hanging out of their mouths
When I am done, little red mouths with no words
Instead no one is so weird
They have muscles
I write these poems instead of sitting in a bed
Sweaty all day
With men who are truly fuckable
I fuck men with muscles, brains, a heart
Men who might listen at times
Not one of them tells jokes about chameleons and armadillos
Like sweet Robbie Wood, who calls me out of the blue
And the one first time I saw him smile, I felt as if
I had been punched in the gut
Oh I know how that one student felt who was in love with me
I say weird things
Weirdness is such a turn-on

THE MOSS PLAY*

Readers and Listeners, you must not be confused. I mean Moss (M-O-S-S), not moth, the bug.

Biography: I called Maggie Sullivan, the little girl I used to babysit and tomorrow we are going to meet for lunch and at 1 o'clock and I lied I did not call her because her mother hates me. Once Maggie Sullivan's brother was my true love. I have never let go of my true love for him. And his mother's voice, acid on the phone, I have never let go of that either.

(Enter the moss play.)

Scene one: The moss sits and grows.
The moss is green, ashy green and
There are red and blue birds flying
And landing on the moss.

(Enter the old soldier)

The old soldier: I am not old. Even as they tear down my house and the moss grows on it, I will not age. As the moss decomposes my eyes and grows over my bones, I will not eat ice-cream. I will not grow old.

Biography: They are tearing down my house. When I was two we moved into this house and I have lost everything here, except my virginity. My virginity they took from me out in the back, Maggie Sullivan's brother and her other brother and her father and the grandfather, too, God rest his soul.

Scene two: When moss heats one expects pea soup, but moss is not peas. Moss is not is not peas. Moss is not peas, it is linen. It is linen and moss is small green flowers that keep growing.

The old solider: And when moss keeps growing, then I will die, my brain a pea soup. My brain is already a blood soup. My body a bone soup and the blood of my body is the red complement to the moss. My red blood complements the green moss. And when I die my red blood will be green. And when I die my old face will be green.

Biography: I wrote Stephanie Young a letter. I think Stephanie Young's about the sweetest girl I've ever seen. I think Stephanie Young the sweetest girl I've ever I've ever...

Scene three:

Maggie Sullivan: I am the moss!
Maggie Sullivan (the double): I am the moss!

Biography: The heart grows like moss and that is all I will ever say about that. I want to go into the past, the warm past. I want to feel the warmth of the past, the past encasing me and making me break. My eyes are glass, and in contained the glass is the eyeball and the God.

Stephanie Young's hair is the kind of hair that is two colors (grey-brown and blond). If she were my friend, I would take her with me onto the boat on the Nevermore. If she were my sister into her I would go.

Scene four: Purple moss is different with a green bird and a yellow sun. All things are inside out. Your outside is your inside.

(The house sways.)

(The house sways and crumbles.)

Biography: There is music playing. I do not know what kind of music it is.

Maggie Sullivan has a voice like her brother's. When I talk to her I pretend I am 16, not 26. I pretend I am 26, a fortune of 16, plus 10 years of love. I pretend we are painting our nails and she is 10. I pretend she is 10 and I am 26. I pretend I am 10 and she is 12. I pretend I am an infant and she is 26.

O how the world turns under!

ELIZABETH TREADWELL

A THOUSAND VIRGINS SHOUT FUCK OFF

to the indie filmmakers carving youth's particulars with their gnarly todds even
while portraying the multitudes
as merely disgusting protrusions of existence & commerce,
even as their own onionskins over their hypnotic guts.

in heaven, a thousand wallflowers shout fuck off across the dance floor,
in heaven, why

because gwyneth paltrow is not that great,
and neither is uma thurman

are you writing your name?

a thousand virgins shout fuck off
to the men of religionto the men and women of god

TROLLS

generic dark-haired girl golden, you kill me, let the talkies get blurry, complicit
mini, snuffalufai vixen, my ass
so I should dress like pretzels or something, ghosts of translucent white gloves,
get blurry as the jester's chair, cast my hair on the water court, existential,
make allowances for spills, nevermind about the fish, my hands uncurled from
their clinging-place, oh gosh, over the waves of the bond jacking cog, forgive me
yet, primeval tricycle, I love you more than her head tilted chic,
spoon out the realism, dunce, I could not solve the cosmic sniggly,
the teepee clickable jester hump

for my sister Carol

ALSOSPACE

dedication to giant grotto recreation of ussong the camera xo. arrival of the prophesied *pucelle*, the virgin messiah of mediaeval lore, called upon to say whatever you need to about whether xo. battle feeling very fucked and reflection on which immeasurably enhanced a causesong a bottle trouble for those who sought to too. totally reading about yon good. yes we know. but the comedy individualizes rather than makes. yes cliqueishness always carry, sword, upward summitswoon, or could scan the happy xo. the person as a key element. epic way you tease out penitentially under a self-proposed somnolence for the past eleven years in her, and thereby stands as testimony amongst example xo. earlier in the modern period. can't on the scene x for o. not previous interim, we know, xo. conclude not entirely nomenclature, the strong utopian and fantastic of so many repressive sumptuary laws at the throne, of the transparent silk veil, further unless about xo xo xo wasn't going, but since you soon wanted directly as not seemed stranger could affect our. please understand harksong. certainly aware of the there is no need for me. to argue about fashion as well as ontological fantasies were misogynist, neither letters nor the greatest artemis. the other thing which throwback chair strokes me about. opposite in gallery, but god for an hour. xo that interiority fought behind mediaeval gaze, up in an alcove of her own so, at the rate go through flotsam devout peasant girl. you cannot have an ideal grace. whose military competence seemed the greatest irony of all to the worldly courtpoet. that great reservoir my curiosity function xo. urine, pots and pans, and roses. an afternoon if we need it, despair happy here. cancel lot, the calves in our meadow. not without dignity, quiet air, semblance gathered. be vexing every misery. a heroine decides when and with whom she. one last phrasesong makes you feel not value my. my. at speaking to actually very more awkward. completely. odd solitary abbey cell translations, always thought, moneywise to you was yours as you did xo. my local relationship to have thought. in setting the theocracy of the seashore. or the wind that blows to the harbor. that would have been enough. this marking much room in everything, and hate such dismay. prefer intervals. late in the count on your fulsome news: dear mrs text in the livesong, xo

from "VIRGINIA OR THE MUD-FLAP GIRL"

[from the crowngirl in shed 20]

from the crowngirl in shed 20

when sweeter hearts prevail

eating shit patties

not so obvious a legend

buried in logic

grasping at straws

in our taskmask,
crown girl

Entertown: circus stool, clown mama, the royal jelly

in the protection groves

the curled lip of the ensoul

PATIENCE, IMOGENE

a clown dripped in heaven

        sensitive fox

the social impact of this

back-bent paradisio, horse-drawn   --

                  (mishap)

————————

indication of fraught begonias, a back-door jewel
(not supposedly here with me)

————————

(your) serenades tired & restless

        a fine place to be

lain, stored in
           (a commentary of daggers)
     thickly tunneled landscape of a former guest

——

-- to what turn-on, knock-kneed allegory
              (barely written/

                   visible)

it is so hard to fall in a clear blue lake

————————

reputations are made on such -- look at her fancy shoes

Donkeyskin One: held in her mouth, the orifice stick of her landlady's chapel, her maid and lady-in-waiting. What she was. Kill the thing. The thing itself shits jewels. And father hid in his quest, hid is quest. A proposition. Trembled little lacy. Girl in the courtyard. In the former wear of snakeskin boots. Land upon her, eyes of dear prince. Charmed, I'm sure, as long as there are grandmothers. And volumes of Perrault.

THE LOVERS OF PETRA SLOVEN

The doors to her innards were imagined by them in rich and flapping detail. "Oro!" screamed one. "Neverland!" another. And yet one more just grunted.

The curves of her lanes were perceived by them through grin of bra and panty. Some days a tiger paw, others nude, still others a classic black.

The cascade of her voice was muted to some, shrill for others, for others omnivalent. The promenade of her nails was sharp for some, bendy for others, for others still unnoticed.

The grip of her legs was loose for some, violent others, others ordinary. The swing of her eyes was mercenary for some, others found them wanting, or superb.

The lines of her orchard were strict for some, for some they were fence-sitting; still others found them floaty.

The grapes of her leaves were poison for some, narcotic others, uppers still for others, others still plain boozy (a few report 'psychodynamic').

The cherry flavored nipples of her to some appeared as pig snouts.

The birthmarks and other marks were left unmapped by some, others dug roads and trenches, for some in daydream she was their palimpsest.

GERALDINE KIM

from POVEL

"'NO!' my cousin says to me as I mix the contents of his cologne bottles. My parents were going to name me after the patron saint of fertility. Then when I came out, they saw that I didn't have a dick. 'Peepeepeepeepee,' I say to my brother as I run past him while we're running on the local track. He just pissed in the woods. Laughing when I saw him climb the snowy hill, looking for a place to yellow the snow.

"Driving past the house where my classmate killed himself. A small red bow decorates the front door. Hugging my dad. 'Wha?' my dad asks as I hug him. 'Life is short,' I say. 'Life is short that's why all last night you hanky-panky,' my mom says. 'What? I was out with my friends last night and I came back by midnight!' I say. 'She got it,' my mom says to the TV screen featuring a woman catching the thief that stole her purse.

"'You're so fucking fake,' I say to the tree branches, just so I would be able to write it here. My brother tells me our mom has started watching *Roseanne*. A rosary in her pocket. How Leibniz must have felt.[181] Driving at night with my friend, looking at people's Christmas decorations. Two houses are facing each other, replete with ornamentation. One with a large inflatable Santa, the other with a large inflatable snowman wearing a scarf, both illuminated against the dark snow. 'What's the word for something that just doesn't belong?' my friend says.

"My hands are cupping my breasts like two small grapefruits. Who am I kidding. More like two oranges. A momentary assessment followed by increasing self-doubt. 'I think they're fine,' my ex once said. Staring at a fish tank filled with goldfish. How did that one goldfish get so much bigger than the others? I wonder. It pushes the other goldfish away with its fins and eats the rest of the food. 'You know how some girls just know how to manipulate guys and guys can't seem to see it but girls can? I'm trying to think of someone from WA[182] that's like that,' my friend says, 'How can guys not see through girls like that?' 'The cause must be their dicks standing between them,' I say.

"We drive by the Roast Beef Sandwich Shop on Gold Star Boulevard. 'That used to be O'Brien's Religious Shop,' I say. 'I know, I read it in your story,' my friend says.[183] Having a dream where my dad gets angry at me since I didn't make curfew at eleven. 'Since when do I have curfew at eleven?' I ask in my dream. 'You've always had curfew at eleven,' my dad says. I kept turning off the air conditioning because I read it was bad for the environment.

"Going back home after church. My mom pulls to the side of the road and starts pummeling me with her hands. Like a windmill. Another car pulls up behind us and knocks on my mom's window. 'What're you doing? You can't hit her like that! That's child abuse. I could call the police! Hey, honey, are you all right?' the stranger says to me. My head is nodding and my cheeks are wet. 'You shouldn't hit your children, that's terrible. You better promise me you'll never hit her again,' he says to my mom. My mom says, 'Okay' and then he drives off.

"Explaining to my ex's brother what is on my shoulder. 'I don't think you're weird, I just think your mom's weird,' he says. Synecdoche would be useful here. "Ew ew this tastes so nasty ew ew" then I've eaten the whole thing,' my brother says. When I thought my goldfish would survive but it kept spinning on the bubbles coming from the filter. Placing my keys atop my ex's mom's Christmas card. 'She's so nice,' my brother said to the card.

"'Why is it funny I'm serious,' my brother says, 'You notice things. I say funny stuff all the time. You're just writing it down, huh?' Then he says, 'Isn't chess racist?' 'Everything's racist,' I say, then laugh. 'What do you mean? Okay: white *before* black. Ughhh this is so nasty I'm gonna eat it anyway,' my brother says. My friends agree I should be a talk show host after I tell them about how I deleted my bass teacher's email to me. Deflecting compliments through bashing on *Oprah*.

"'I'm getting into hardcore. It's funny; you can't take it seriously,' I say to my friend. My brother and I are watching *Days of Our* Lives. 'The acting's so horrible. Where's Stefano?[184] I love how there are like three thousand plots and all of them suck. . . And how do they get fortunes in fortune cookies?' my brother says. Then a soap opera in Spanish with captions. 'They can afford captions?' my brother says, then laughs.

"'I'm a dancer and I know he didn't produce the number one dance CD,' a guy with pointy/gelled hair says on TV with the word 'choreographer' on the bottom. 'This goes out to all the firefighters and policemen that lost their lives on September 11,' the singer says, then starts screaming, 'I DID IT!!!'[185] Then I say, 'She's like a god to you, incapable of doing anything.'

"'Madden[186] knows what plays I'm doing now; I hate those advanced systems,' my brother says to me. 'All men are dogs,' my mom says. I ask if that includes my brother and father. 'All men are dogs,' my mom says again. We were driving on Shrewsbury Street, talking about birth control. 'It's like, you know you're being irrational in the back of your mind,' I say. Buying the new Pinhead Gunpowder CD and calculating that each song costs $1.09.

"My mom asks to read my novel so far. Telling my brother she wouldn't get it, not even the parts about her clutching rosaries. 'Is your mom okay with you calling me mom?' my ex's mom's email says. Driving in the fog. Deciding to get my mom clothes from Lane Bryant[187] at the Greendale Mall for a holiday present. Immediately feeling insecure about my body size. I'm shopping for my mom, not for me, I want to say to the pictures of smiling fat models on the walls, the large shirts folded in neat towers.

"Can I help you?' her averted eyes say. 'It's for my mom,' I add. She offers a 'chocolaty-colored' pair of pants and my mouth saying, 'fine.' 'Sorry, ma'am, I'm gonna have to ring you up after her,' the plump register woman says to the even plumper mother behind me. Her daughters are looking at me. You're thin. . . *for now*. So fucking paranoid. 'It's 20 percent off if you get the card,' her large breasts say. One large velour sweatshirt has 'Sporty' written in blue rhinestones. Behind the register is a box of TaffyTaffy with empty wrappers inside.[188]

"Vowing to do crunches and sit-ups as soon as I get home. We were reminiscing about our absent friend. How he is probably going to marry his thirty-plus-year-old boyfriend on the Cape. 'It's so fucking depressing there the rest of the year,' I say, 'No wonder so many writers live there.' "Who was that writer's house we saw there?' my friend asks. 'Eugene O'Neill,' I say. A sign advertising New & Used Automobiles lined by blue neon light. Telling my friend how that sign represents our friend's life.

"Deciding to delete all the proper names of people in this text. Not counting public figures. This song doesn't have a refrain. When rappers put movie skits in or bleep out swears by inserting the electronic blipblip of car remote recognition. As soon as the other runner left the track, I felt I could run in peace. Counting how many laps I run makes time go slower than if I don't pay attention.

"And not doing them. I planned a story about a painter and a photographer.[189] It would have been about a still-life painter who was seeing a female photographer. And as soon as she saw the painting of herself, she would have seen a disgusting frog instead and looked at herself in a mirror and she would indeed have been a frog. Then she would have leaped away and become the trees and dirt she saw.

"If I ran around this track without stopping, all night. The sunset reminds me of my sister. We were visiting Venice Beach together and there was trash in the sand. 'That was fast,' I said to her. He replaces 'reading' with 'writing.' Have the last word. Asking my mom about the miscarriage between my sister and me. 'Did you have an abortion?' she asks me. Someone already wrote a poem cursing the rising sun.

"'You never move your back row!' my brother says to me about playing checkers. 'King me,' I say. Then add more pieces atop the crowned piece to create a tower. Teaching myself Mandarin. My friend laughing at me, 'That's not how you say it! It's *èr*,' My vocal imitation like a deflating balloon. 'You're such a douche,' my brother says. 'Since when do you use the word 'douche'? Someone probably called you a douche and you've just been saving it to use against someone,' I say. 'No, you're just a douche,' my brother says.

"My brother's hands moving the checker-pieces and his mouth saying, 'That's how Yahoo! plays it.' The amusement park claimed that you would have 'a whale of a time' there.[190] My brother's friend invited himself and slashed the tires of our car with his pocket-knife. He lived with his grandmother. How we hated each other so much yet wouldn't leave the Spider ride because both of us wanted to stay in our seats for a second time.

"Our history teacher kept addressing me by my older sister's name. The year my brother started going to school with me, I told him to not talk to me in public. 'They need to dim the lights in here,' I say as we walk into the restaurant, 'I feel so exposed.' 'Your cousin got into medical school,' my parents tell me. Remembering the first and only time I visited Korea and my cousin, who I had never met, staying in her room/ not greeting us because she had finals that week. And her sister/ my retarded cousin sitting in the room with us with her tilted head and soft moaning sounds.

"'Good for her,' I say. Her older brother had autism. Her other older brother was valedictorian of his class. 'They look alike,' I said to the picture frame. My brother comes into my room just to tell me he wrestled our dad. 'Wanna wrestle?' he asks me. To stay overnight at a mall.[191] Trying to form mathematical relationships between the numbers on the clock. $9 = 3^2$. $9 = 3 \times 3$. Fuck. Fuck. $9 = 3 + 6$. 'John Ritter died,' my brother says to the TV. 'Who cares,' I say. A Sinatra song on the computer. 'Britney Spears sang this on Starch Shirts,' my brother says.

"The TV shows a 125-year-old fruitcake on Jay Leno. Exams had just finished and I finally found my brother. 'What took you so long?' I ask him. 'What?' he says. 'What took you so long?' I say again. 'I wanted to focus so I took some of

Ryan's Ritalin,' my brother says. My dad telling me about the son of a news anchor that suddenly died. 'Who cares. Three kids killed themselves at school,' I say. 'Yes, hut this boy was a good kid,' my dad says.

"Three pages left. Dunno why I try so hard. 'Then you'd have to assume all matter is conscious,' my ex's email says. Or you could just assume our consciousness is matter, I want to say. If I had said it, I would have entitled that email, 'Re: Fwd: falling into collapsible chairs.' A blanket hides the lower half of his face.

"A T-shirt that would say, 'I've made it this far, haven't I?' He was white and her parents were Korean. 'Then why did you guys break up?' I ask my cousin. Death is coming and I'm debating whether or not I need to re-coat my nails. 'You like this music? It's so bad,' my brother says. 'Yeah, it's funny,' I say. 'Are they serious?' my brother asks. Yeah, that's what makes it funny,' I say.

"The computer is humming. How I thought the shampoo/conditioner bottles for Normal Hair' signified the desired condition for hair. Which was why I didn't understand the need for 'Dry' or 'Oily.' The only story I remember from the collection is 'Hannah is a Palindrome,' and in the end, the main character says, 'Otto is a palindrome,' to her classmate/tormentor. The toilet seat is up and droplets of pee on the floor. 'Just aim your dick into the bowl!' I say to the toilet.

"Write a song over vacation. And my sudden desire to smoke cigarettes. Planning to smoke one after I run for the day. 'Don't talk,' my dad says to my mom when I tell her I don't want to eat anything. My brother is laughing and listening to Shai Hulud with the lyrics in his hand and says, 'I lost my place.' 'Everything swear,' my mom says when she comes into the room.

"I don't know really—sometimes you know what you're doing and then I don't know,' my dad says to me. The least favorite word was 'used.' Am I that different-looking with this haircut? What gay men think of women. 'I'm sick of Madonna,' I say. 'Me too,' my friend says. Staying silent because it reminds us of our friend. Imagining a skyscraper with each floor being different: the first floor with just toilets, the second floor with soap, the third with sinks, the fourth with towels.

"Dreaming my ex and I are with a bunch of friends watching a movie. And I'm just wearing a red shirt and thong. We run into the dark theater and I feel so lonely being with everyone there. The bagel store with a twenty-five-cent bagel sale on Mondays. And an old woman leaving the store with a bag of bagels the size of her torso. My mom wakes me up just to say 'Merry Christmas,' then closes the door. It is Christmas Eve.

"Now that I had the track entirely to myself I didn't have to think about passing him or calculating my pace in relation to his. White jet exhaust cutting the sky like orange skin bleeding white. 'Are you one of those types that looks down on people that don't listen to Indie?' I asked my ex when we were starting to go out. 'No . . .' he said. 'You couldn't have heard of it,' he said when I told him I had heard of Dynamite Kid. I meant Kid Dynamite.

"'That whole "I'm more Marxist than thou" attitude,' my roommate says. Remembering how my ex got pissed when I said I was a socialist. 'If you really were a socialist, you wouldn't even be here,' he said. 'Here' meaning college I suppose. When we started saying 'Fine fine' to each other. Dreading my sister's arrival. No email. 'Did you make that up?' I ask. 'No, I heard it from someone else,' she says.

"She would always call people she didn't like a 'waste of space.' I wanted to add. 'And *time* too!' The reason why I gave up any hope of becoming a stand-up comedian. Telling my friends about how my friend's dad said I looked like a vampire. 'Oh I thought it was a little kid,' my ex says. Meant to be taken as a joke. The words 'MENSA' and 'Historical Interpreter' in my notebook and I have no idea what I'm supposed to be reminded of from that.

"Realizing I already wrote that. When I used to think there was a relationship between 'heroin' and 'heroine.' Someone leaves an orange traffic cone, Worcester

DPW sign, and a stop sign on our front porch. 'It's like a racial slur, that's a bigotry,' my dad says. 'It's funny,' I say, 'they're prolly just kids.' 'I don't think so!' my dad says. My brother talking about taking a shotgun and shooting whoever it was between the eyes. '*That'd* be funny,' he says and my dad agreeing with him.

'"Four-year-old-girl ding dong,' my dad says, telling us about the time he caught a girl ringing our doorbell for fun. 'I saw another adult there,' my mom says. My psychology textbook about mixing sources in memory. How my dad waited for the next time a prankster rang the doorbell. 'For four consecutive days I wait. It was around nine o'clock,' my dad says. 'It's not like they're putting dead fetuses on our door or throwing rocks through our windows,' I say. 'They're gonna do that next,' my dad says sternly.

'"Haha yeah I want a gift certificate to Picadilly Pub for Christmas,' my brother says to the billboard. 'Death certificate, birth certificate,' my dad says. 'Why do you always think of death and life,' my brother says. Confusing speakers. 'Yeah a *wet* Christmas. It's like Santa is peeing on us,' my brother says. We were in a concert hall decorated by naked Grecian figures. The gay singer I had a crush on said before, They're...kinda small, huh?'

'"You guys should just divorce,' I say to my dad. The world as genitals. Giving a blowjob to my ex while his mom drove the van back to his house. '*Leno* means pimp in Latin like Jay Leno,' my brother says. The words 'Creative Writing' written on the back of my notebook. 'They used to rub dog shit on their faces to show grief,' my brother says. Envision the entire family dying while driving in this van.

"Telling my brother about the fights I had with my ex. 'You shouldn't make stuff a big deal,' my brother says. 'It's raining dog and cat,' my mom says to the windshield wipers. 'Stop touching my *hind*,' my dad says to my brother. 'Say it in Latin,' my brother says. 'Gluteus maximus!' says my dad. 'It smells like urea in here,' I say to my mom's coffee cup.

[181] When Newton and Leibniz both "discovered" calculus, Newton got the credit for it since his methodology was easier to follow.

[182] Worcester Academy

[183] There used to be a small shop on Gold Star Boulevard that sold religious merchandise. Its title was "O'Brien's Religious Shop" and a middle-aged Irish couple owned it. Occasionally I would have to accompany my mother on these mini-pilgrimages in order to sate her unending desire for God's acceptance. I give you my word, dear reader, as soon as my mother discontinued her commerce at that establishment due to my father's early retirement, the religious shop promptly went out of business. A roast-beef sandwich shop has since taken its place.

[184] Stefano is an evil character on the soap opera.

[185] "I.D.S. (Live)" by Sworn Enemy.

[186] Madden 2003, a football video game on Sony Playstation that my brother plays with seeming religious ferocity.

[187] "Plus size" women's clothing store

II. TO BE READ PRIVATELY:

the dirty clothes
are going to
be clean soon.
hot laundromats have
no air but are full

of sodium
light.vibrating
washing
machines are arous
ing when sat upon. it

is quite pos
sible to sh-rin
k to the size of
a molec-ule
of oxygen float

ing in this
static space and
not thin-king these
dirty thoughts.

HEIDI LYNN STAPLES

DAMSEL IN UNDRESS

How nice it is to be broken!
Because really, it's no abuse prettifying, one isn't au pair of sex till broken into is one?
I mean falls down a peep hole cocked.

Quiet! Shatter joyfully as the stick and the glass.
The terrible is the body as a locket, the pictures inside a fool and a bully; as we are, just as broken.

That's so pock-marked! People are so pockmarked.
For example, she wants her body aimed at its target market.
She wants to be a door able, a man's true fool filled
meat, his lost and most pirated possession.

JUST PUSH ME INTO THE WATER SO I CAN FLOAT

this woman contains information about the possibility that falling into the water may lower your thirst. the woman also suggests that the orange dress and bright silver hair barrette may heighten your thirst. throughout the woman it does seem that the concrete slab is favored, the orange dress and bright silver hair barrette, mainly because of the face down thirst from falling into the water, o there maybe lights bespangledness. you may be those who are afraid. who are frayed with fear. they are a thirst with their currents. they include water.

sore are those who quest toward the ever.
life is hard.
the other a rippling surface.
so much in motion beneath with teeth.

the orange dress and bright silver hair barrette. the slab is a whale a mollusk knows the all she knows. grown. thrown onto. an exposed thigh. the white is very easy to wander in and the woman is quite easy to dream, and should be hopeful for those who are taking her as their own personal souvenir. senses my world and souvenir. face down a toe in the water between the orange dress and the bright silver hair barrette verses falling into the water, i think that this woman is a struggling hopeful.

LITERAL OF APPARITION

I am applying for the position of it; see fig. My qualifications include a year spanned as a gratuitous fissure, during which time I as in the meshes of the wet; style of slip: artsy-heartsy project. With a day green in veneration, I wouldn't arrange a thing. OK, maybe I wed.

My responsibilities include an uneasy, the her person nude thrill. I have significant. I have experience and many other silky underlings. This is how it unfolded. It's that isostasy I wean. The different forks in the here ended up her. Also, the sound amphibolous. My mind altered, ample was so formed.

I am planning nipples supplanting napalms. I am a girl, and I said 'pink'. I am a girl, and I said 'eat me raw'.

References disabled disown the nest.

FONDER A CARE KEPT

I was barn. I was razed.

I was mot this flame with no's sum else blue's blame noir yearning down the house.

No, it was I and I blank I bandit blather that louse that fiddle-dee-dee little lame chimera that came as the name yes different.

I wracked my refrain, that blousy souse.

I was bard. I was crazed.

I was dog girl's shame.

So, I culled my maim. My maze read, you heave to rip rove your aim (she knock knocks my nows and raves my here a quickened tousle), spell your dreams with a big and, and play for the game.

I was har. I was phrase.

I was aroused by many's uttered same.

MARGIC

Try this: As we heave dawn with the consistent shimmer sex ample example, compose a winsome dimple instance and then a verily writhing sex pants expansions: a come pound me subject me, a come pound me prettily, a come pound me sex instance, a come pound me come sex me sex instance. To pretty lend this sex exercise ram, coming, he's so moanly, I'm my cunt-and-all, keep him in. How deferent sex instances shapely lust. Accomplice, deferent rear-end. In other words, make lure that your come pound me sex instance balances to I'm in. Of in, form elation. That your come sex me sex instance emphasizes moan's zing and unzip, it's zowie, kerpow!, pining's p.o.w. arching in formed ache's elations sing-a-longing (in the moan, claw). And that your come pound me come sex me sex instance is its blown reworld. Gift roam own your moans and needs rite now.

LILITH OF THE EARLY MONIKERS

And so near the fierce rest, whole body nod,
the opposite of a dive, her odd ministering
angles from on top, he's would in her.

They look from a certain perspective
like a snail. *What is all this?* he shouts,
How about like this? Shouting starts

flare there what noise. Speaking in cymbals
in wonder grand caverns. The moan spins
enormous, her legs hallelu, flat

on her back, a mother unborn
when needs point up, he's between her legs
(now it's like he got wings) *No! Know! Gno!*

she exclaimed, struck out, unweddingly
broke his noose. *My museum!* he wept.

KIM ROSENFIELD

DAUGHTERS OF GENIUS *from* "DAUGHTERS OF GENIUS"

KIMBERLY ROSENFIELD, WE'VE BEEN LOOKING FOR YOU!
We are bleeding arterially…Girlhood
Mrs. L.M. Monmouth and how she lived on 40 dollars a year.

WOMEN ECCENTRIC & PECULIAR:

Victory through the tunnel-you call it womb-
The want of furniture-the children neglected-
Makes a man of him-his opinion of her-reforms the household-his
gratitude to her-
Her opinion of him-her grave…

THE MILK DISEASE:

Green boards
She was given to vicissitudes
They ate steak off copper plates.

She was an invalid until she met RB
Shoes sewn from flannel strips-corn meal-oat meal-salt pork-
molasses
Dome parties at Vassar-a pretty sitting room
Chiefest symptoms died away-different from the political
The Tempter takes
Flung-back frock coat-and people like me may well
ask themselves
His wife died young
Deeper shade-lively liberalism.

THE WANDERING UTERUS *from* "DAUGHTERS OF GENIUS"

"and now, O woman, we call upon thee to help thyself"

Miss Wiggles is a sensitive
large quantity of limpid urine
the most abundant crop of fruit
heavily disguised as venereal passion
noises in the head, glowing balls of light.

Insufflations.

Slow interrupted breathing, turgid neck, flushed cheek.

Proverbially erotic, egotistical, and religious
nasal feeding
charnel house smell.

Dreaming, ETC.
Waking and sleeping, ETC.
Spectral lights, ETC.

EXCELSIOR REFLECTOR FROM "TRAVELS WITH A DONKEY: EXCELSIOR REFLECTOR"

Designs in Poetry for a Fashion Spring Forecast (Post Valentine's Day Massacre)

STORY OF A DRESS:

Super/ revealing
violently/ form fitting
asymmetrical cutaway gown.

In this dress/ I felt like/ a woman.

You have to/ stand up straight/
throw out/ your shoulders
and lean/ into the dress.

You have to/ hold your champagne glass/
a certain way.

You don't need/ a bra
the dress/ holds it/
all together/ for you.

Pressed crepe underwear options
(Brown being the new black)
(Red being the new neutral).

Backless, strapless
sheer net bra
slash-front
bust-boosting body slips.

Cotton briefs are like meeting in the rainforest
no longer just for girls being killed going to school
An American Classic
The future
never looked so
re-affirming.

Please hear this as pure fashion information
direct from the runways, as the designers intended:

Not all voices/in fashion/are calling/is back
Consider the centrality of macro ruffles
to a woman's spring existence.

Runway looks are all about _____
It is a_____season in NYC, full of_____
and_____ and in keeping with that mood the bog
news is:
Peaches for breakfast! Then golf! Then a swim!

Be a Pavlova and nothing else!

Kohl-rimmed eyes and a total lack of discretion
handsome faces half-hidden in the shadows of the night

The frayed places on your pink kimona.
[Musical Interlude}

(Sung in a small voice)

Buy yourself a white dress
with a lovely sash,
an ashes of roses sash,
as pale and crystalline
as a Greek ocean—
and buy yourself
a leghorn hat—and you will be
as picturesque as a summer path
over the mead-ow.

This inner settlement feels like
unhappiness, sluggish apathy,
and hopeless, helpless boredom.

CAN'T "MAKE IT" WITH YOUR PARENTS?

Pervasive self-dislike follows her here
"I was still a little girls,
I was getting breasts, you know."

VERY DOWN WHEN YOU WAKENED THIS MORNING?

ARE YOU FEELING, PERHAPS, THAT YOU'RE A <u>NO GOOD</u> PERSON?
The unwitting burlesque of base female crime
An ever ready & waiting Xerox machine
My own Blueprint for Heaven.

Leaving your shame, she breathed deeply
he felt some shame in surveying the unclad women.

Take the lid off/ your relationship/ potential
When I learned to/ enjoy the/ raw feelings of/ you body.

Child adrift in the world herself
Novel hormonal status, household spells
MGM spectacular
You know, something to with her own life.
Being me-for-them at the end of a yo-yo.

Ask yourself what they all have in common,
and you see, they know the following:

You get/ the cold shoulder
If you're not/ wearing gown.

Shoes cobbled over so thickly
Hose hanging over his huggers
Miserable mittens made of old rags
Fingers worn out and filth clotted on them
A clouted coat cut short to the knee.

3 yards of purple shamlet
A bonnet of deep murray
A hose of yellow kersey
Laces of silk
Mink cuffs.

The first woman to be a man of letters.

[Sex is a red-blooded thing—
into it she dumped her paint pots]

STEP OUT A BIT WITH A SNAPPY GIGOLO
OR A NEIGHBOR WHOSE WIFE DOESN'T UNDERSTAND HIM.

Having to do with being an individual's
individual creation.

No G-strings, NUDE!

_____wears a gown
of rich brown taffeta
lined with shimmering gold lame.

From her shoulders
extends a curve
a soft, silky velvet
perfectly complimented
by a

three-tiered tiara.
Golden embroidery and sparkling sequins
swirl together elegantly
at the foot of
her gown
and her blonde hair
is swept up in
curls.

WHAT DO THEY THINK WE DO ON BOY'S NIGHT OUT?

Beauty provides grounding in getting a life
for those of us not blessed in the cradle
spurred by guilt of excess
stuffed full of celebrity food
ravaged by expensive alcohol
Please! Cover that mirror!

Memorandum to Self:

CHAPTER 14 FROM "RE: EVOLUTION"

(you are what you think you are)
Saying "no" to everything is a
Crucial way to be assured that
One is really themselves
(The "I" is still a child).

Economy as waste product
Do we have a chance to be better?
A second chance?

When the baby enters the birth canal
Does a disembodied spirit go in and pull
A switch-a-roo?

What happens when you like the merchandising
More than the man?

"State-dependent recall."

Pity toward another version of the self.

Emotions are culturally
And historically
Specific.

Ennui, angst, amai, being a wild pig
Desirable, contemptible, admirable, despicable, respectable.

"Maternal thinking"
People who were diseased with this default.

Why was I borne? When I was borne?
Why was I given
The body I'm livin' in?[12]

Klonapin, Wellbutrin, Lexapro, Lamictal,
Effexor, Prozac, Celexa, Zoloft, Ambien.

Decorum, gravity, and norm making
Clowning, parody, and norm breaking.

Masculinized sorrow
Everlasting virginity
Black Register of a Thousand Sins
Ontological and essentialist
He-Whore.

B. went through the forest of being
But is coming out of the lake of knowing.

Networks, meeting sites, body language.

Who has the power to establish a version of the self?

Jane never doubted why she needed to hate Charles.

It's not true to be so good
Now goodbye daughter!
A masterpiece in the medical style.

[12] Sung like a show tune*

I buried myself alive.

It's not a fancy yesterday.

So many beings I know I could be me in.*

! Genderlicious Genderbars !

One individual? Or several?

Chromosomal similarity is
Not an all-or-nothing affair.

The cultural heredity of a human population.

The cultural heredity of a horse population.

The ultimate extension of the ancestral family.

Also, the family of the future.

(Genetic endowments of posterity).

(Vermont frogs will never meet Florida frogs).

MATTHEA HARVEY

IDEAS GO ONLY SO FAR

Last year I made up a baby. I made her in the shape of a hatbox or a cake. I could have iced her & no one would have been the wiser. You know how trained elephants will step onto a little round platform, cramming all four fat feet together? That's her too, & the fez on the elephant's head. Applause all around. There was no denying I had made a good baby. I gave her a sweet face, a pair of pretty eyes, & a secret trait at her christening. I set her on my desk, face up, and waited. I watched her like a clock. I didn't coo at her though. She wasn't that kind of baby.

She never got any bigger, but she did learn to roll. Her little flat face went round and round. On her other side, her not-face rolled round and round too. She followed me everywhere. When I swam, she floated in the swimming pool, a platter for the sun. When I read, she was my peacefully blinking footstool. She fit so perfectly into the washing machine that perhaps I washed her more than necessary. But it was wonderful to watch her eyes slitted against the suds, a stray red sock swishing about her face like the tongue of some large animal.

When you make up a good baby, other people will want one too. Who's to say that I'm the only one who deserves a dear little machine-washable ever-so-presentable baby. Not me. So I made a batch. But they weren't exactly like her— they were smaller & without any inborn dread. Sometimes I see one rolling past my window at sunset—quite unlike my baby, who like any good idea, eventually ended up dead.

GOOD-BYE TO IF *from* "CEILING UNLIMITED SERIES"

The plastic pagoda hasn't helped nor have
the pills. Red to green, no sign of yellow.
There's no way to know if you're listening.
Why does two always have to be a tawdry,
fluttering thing? Throw it to the side of the road
& find some other canvas. Let the statues
soften, my hand shadow itself for a change.
Throw your light on the bricks or the cracks
in-between, it won't impress the invalids in
hammocks taking their pulses. They know how
to count. Slice through the bleating & you have
six pairs of smallish gloves, pearls at each wrist.
No one said anything about violet-water or later.
The next time a rhinestone falls to the floor,
you won't find me on my knees.

THE EMPTY PET FACTORY

My love works the night shift at the Empty Pet factory. I've only been there once and I still have nightmares about the heartless hamster he had me hold in my hand, the rooms of inside-out Chihuahuas I saw drying on racks. The pet waitlist keeps getting longer. Celebrities love them. To the outside world you can continue to seem like America's sweetheart, simpering, *I do hope the fox gets away* as you dig your heels into a horse filled to the brim with vitriol and follow the flash of red over the hedge. Only the keenest eye could detect that you just screwed your horse's shiny eyes into its head after emptying handfuls of hate into its big glossy body. This morning, over breakfast, he tells me excitedly that they've perfected the Unrequited Love Puppies—their chubbiness will serve as camouflage for the love bulging and straining against their doubly reinforced seams. He's getting toast crumbs all over his uniform. One lands inside the Empty Pet logo on his lapel—an outline of an indeterminate mammal. The cages stacked in the corners are quiet. The parrots think it's night when the covers are on. They're all factory rejects— couldn't learn to keep quiet the things they've been told. At night, when he's gone, sometimes I turn on all the lights and let them squawk the test secrets they've been fed in the laboratory, a glorious cacophony of *I hate your mother, Your best friend made a pass at me and I never liked your nose.* I think one day he'll come home and find me in there with them, repeating over and over again, *You don't understand me. You never have.*

TO ZANZIBAR BY MOTORCAR

In Regensberg, the cloud
left the mountain. In vain

I crumpled my crinolines,
scuffed the sand outside the temple.

My eyes took in only eye-shaped
things—mouseface flickering

in the mousehole, pansies
twitching with palsy. Where

the squint and the kiss are common,
there are no rebels lurking

between the 15th and 16th parallel.
Children are symmetrical

& zebras fingerprint the plains.
Ask me if I'm pretending

& I will freeze to delineate
my non-nod from my nod.

BAKED ALASKA, A THEORY OF

The moat simmers at 210°. From his tower the king watches, pleased, as a swallow tries to land on the water, squawks & flies off. He believes in setting a good example. *O the flesh is hot but the heart is cold, you'll be alone when you are old*, his favorite country song—on repeat—is being piped through the palace. Downstairs in the dining room, the princesses gaze out the window at a flock of pigeons turning pink then black as they fly in & out of the sunset. The princesses put down their spoons & sigh. Baked Alaska for dessert again. The flambé lights up their downcast faces. In the fireplace, dry ice sizzles didactically. When dinner is over, they return to their wing of the palace, The Right Ventricle. On a good day, they can play Hearts for a few hours before they hear the king's dactylic footsteps (*dámn the queen, dámn the queen*) coming down the aorta & have to hide the cards. They aren't allowed to adore him, so they don't, just allow his inspections—checking their eyes for stars, their journals for heated confessions. Because he is a literal man, he never finds anything. But that night, when he's gone, the princesses tiptoe down to the palace freezer. Sticking their fingers in sockets is no longer enough. Amongst the frozen slabs of beef, they sit in a circle on blocks of ice & watch the red fade from their lips & fingers, the frost on the floor creep up the heels of their shoes. Finally when the skin is numb, the heat starts retreating into their hearts & they can feel it—love, love, love.

THE CROWDS CHEERED AS GLOOM GALLOPED AWAY

Everyone was happier. But where did the sadness go? People wanted to know. They didn't want it collecting in their elbows or knees then popping up later. The girl who thought of the ponies made a lot of money. Now a month's supply of pills came in a hard blue case with a handle. You opened it & found the usual vial plus six tiny ponies of assorted shapes & sizes, softly breathing in the Styrofoam. Often they had to be pried out & would wobble a little when first put on the ground. In the beginning the children tried to play with them, but the sharp hooves nicked their fingers & the ponies refused to jump over pencil hurdles. The children stopped feeding them sugarwater & the ponies were left to break their legs on the gardens' gravel paths or drown in the gutters. On the first day of the month, rats gathered on doorsteps & spat out only the bitter manes. Many a pony's last sight was a bounding squirrel with its tail hovering over its head like a halo. Behind the movie theatre the hardier ponies gathered in packs amongst the cigarette butts, getting their hooves stuck in wads of gum. They lined the hills at funerals, huddled under folding chairs at weddings. It became a matter of pride if one of your ponies proved unusually sturdy. People would smile & say, "This would have been an awful month for me," pointing to the glossy palomino trotting energetically around their ankles. Eventually, the ponies were no longer needed. People had learned to imagine their sadness trotting away. & when they wanted something more tangible, they could always go to the racetrack & study the larger horses' faces. Gloom, #341, with those big black eyes, was almost sure to win.

SHIVER & YOU HAVE WEATHER

Engine: ☑ ☐

In the aftermath of calculus
your toast fell butter-side down.

Squirrels swarmed the lawns
in flight patterns. The hovercraft

helped the waves along. From
every corner there was perspective.

On the billboards the diamonds
were real, in the stores, only zirconia.

I cc'ed you. I let you know.
Sat down to write the Black Ice Memo.

Dinner would be meager &
reminiscent of next week's lunch.

So what if I sat on the sectional?
As always I was beside myself.

IMPLICATIONS FOR MODERN LIFE

The ham flowers have veins and are rimmed in rind, each petal a little meat sunset. I deny all connection with the ham flowers, the barge floating by loaded with lard, the white flagstones like platelets in the blood-red road. I'll put the calves in coats so the ravens can't gore them, bandage up the cut gate and when the wind rustles its muscles, I'll gather the seeds and burn them. But then I see a horse lying on the side of the road and think *You are sleeping, you are sleeping, I will make you be sleeping*. But if I didn't make the ham flowers, how can I make him get up? I made the ham flowers. Get up, dear animal. Here is your pasture flecked with pink, your oily river, your bleeding barn. Decide what to look at and how. If you lower your lashes, the blood looks like mud. If you stay, I will find you fresh hay.

ESTAMOS EN VIVO, NO HAY ALTERNATIVO

Down here in the land of slammed doors,
the factory puffs its own set of clouds

into the sky. Fake larks fly through
them, lifelike. Let's not go into contractions

of can't and won't or how behind the line of trees,
the forest is gone. Dip that tiny brush into

your paintbox and mix up something nice
and muddy for me. We've got a lock

on the moon so now it goes where we want it—
mostly proms, sometimes lobbies.

This is my favorite sign: "Live girls, live action!"
and in smaller but still flashing lights:

"girl on girl, girl on _____." Among the permutations,
there's no "girl on hands and knees begging for her life."

No one we know wants it that badly.

FREE ELECTRICITY

First the prong marks appeared on my cheeks as if someone had scratched equals signs under my eyes. Three days later there was an aching just behind my knee and I found the first socket. I studied it with a hand mirror. It was exactly the shape of the outlet next to my bed—two rectangular openings and below them a hole like the mouth of a tunnel. I can remember the order in which they appeared—one on the side of my neck, another on my shoulderblade, another in the sole of my foot, yet another at my wrist—but I don't remember who first used me. I remember folding up my miniskirts and short-sleeved shirts and wearing clothes that covered every inch, so perhaps it was a lover who discovered my hidden talent—took the alarm clock and plugged it into my foot—or my sister who positioned me close to the blender when the power went out. At first it was just as a favor. "Would you mind…." "Would it be too much trouble…." Etc. But soon they didn't ask. It's all so long ago now—I've grown used to my cocoon of orange cords. Someone kind left a gap at my eyes, so at night I can see the red switches of the piles of power-strips blinking and imagine the city running on whatever strange surge (not quite sugar, not quite caffeine) flows through my veins. That's me in the hum of your fan, me in the crackle of your TV, me lighting up every last lightbulb.

NADA GORDON

from **"FLESHSCAPE"**

To make a cape
of flesh, take
the labia minora
between the thumb
and forefinger, s-t-r-e-t-c-h
downwards and back
over the buttocks, then
upward along the ribcage,
curling them over
shoulders. Using palms,
rub the end flaps
onto the pectorals.
They will stick to the body
surface warmly, smelling
of minerals and cream,
their rosy hue ideal
for summer evenings.

VAGABOND IMPERIALISM

Who isn't envaginated in rhetoric?
Slathered with its perfume, pigs root through
the debris of the 20th century—a scuttling octopus,
a spidery machine, ghosts of ocean rays. Here's an octave
and a cup of bitters, some kohlrabi, and creepy
music box music. **POP** ! Out come the same old
arguments leading to the same old cul de sacs, then **POP**
they all disappear in a shower of gluey sparks, like extreme
plastic surgery performed on wisteria for the sole benefit
of the already-converted.

At least Gaptoothed Helen dances to the level of her eyeliner.
And Asha Bhosle, in a mirrored choli, lets loose with the heavy breathing.

SHE SURE LIKES THE CREAM

sayonara.
fleurdelys.
cherry twinklemall.
princess.
human hair and glass eyes
mischief kreme.

I have dream(s)! dreamy-girl
Magic the kitty cat Sweet Kitty,
Paper Panache paper-piecing patterns
My Dog Spot/ Sweet Kitty Dreams.
My Dog Spot, Sweet Kitty Dreams.

Shiva Cat Slave to the Dance Sweet-Kitty.
[The Pink Power] Cliques: *Meu
What a SWEET kitty! What a SWEET kitty!
Darling little cathead with a pretty little bow
around its neck. Three Sweet Kitty Babies
NothingKitty acting like a sweet Kitty

NothingKitty acting like a sweet
Human hair and glass eyes, SWEET KITTY
He is a sweet kitty, but can also be rather moody.
Sweetie is exactly that—a very sweet kitty.
Aww, Sweet Kitty. Oh My God!

Come pet my kitty sweet kitty
Yes, those with Empathy you like kitties
you're nice you care Kitties are nice electric ferret

DOES YOUR SWEET KITTY LOOK AT YOU LIKE THIS
WHEN ASKED TO OBEY? My Little Kitty
This is my sweet kitty Shadow. Finding Ugly
In Wolf, a reminder of our mortality

tuffy dog purrs all the time.
My dear Auntie BamBam, I love you too,
from Phelicity Sweet Kitty. Snuggles.
This is Snuggles. I really am a sweet kitty
with a lot of love to give –
Won't YOU let me show YOU how sweet I am??

I am a very sweet kitty who is a little on the shy side.
I really am quite stunning.
I like to pose in front of the camera
and to show my body on the net.
Kitty lose myself in your cotton fur
Good kitty Put me to sleep with your Nice kitty

Sweet Kitty Kiss my ghosts Kitty doesn't like
the soup, Mama, but she sure likes the cream.
Sweet kitty, where'd she go? Scratchy tongue
and tiny wet nose. Sweet kitty, where you been?"
Mares. Tijuana Pine Tijuana Moonshine Lady Sugar
Blue Bubbles. "Come kitty kitty Come home

sweet kitty Come my sweet little Kitty."
Come home sweet kitty Come to me Kitty kitty."
SWEET KITTY,HOT MIKO, WILD HAZMY.
SWEET KITTY, HOT MIKO, WILD HAZMY.
My sweet kitty Parameter, my parrot Diogenes

Kitty, O Kitty, Your sweet more than the rest.
Kitty, sweet kitty. Your simply the best.
ANXIETY ATTACK! ANXIETY ATTACK!
to be entirely stable. Sweet sweet kitty,
until she decides she's not
and lets you know it.

MY ETERNAL DILEMMA

My Eternal Dilemma... I think I have ADD And no one loves me. And I annoy my friends a lot. And no one loves me. And I think I'm starting to hate men.

No-one loves me! No-one loves me! guava says... As i'm sure you've not asked everyone, how can you know this is true?

Everyones in love these days!! Everyone except me, that's cos no one loves me.

No-one loves me like Jesus loves me In his arms I'm happy No-one knows me like Jesus knows me No-one knows like he knows No-one loves like he loves He loves

I love my dog, because my dog is where I have hidden my love, no one loves me at all! They command me. But no one loves me!

I only do these things because no-one loves me and my life is dull.

no one loves, me's Blurty

No one loves me like my tomato can

This is the level of philosophies, conclusions, and assumptions, such as, "No one loves me."

Why they don't notice me. Why I can't tell them how I feel. Why no one loves me. And no matter how hard I try, they'll never see.

I often feel that no one loves me. If I have problems,

I have to tackle them on my own. At the moment, I feel like an outcast.

Who can understand me if I cant understand my self? No one cares for me. No one loves me. I don't love my self. I am the dust swept under the rug.

Runaway. I want to runaway. But where would I go? No one would take me in, no one loves me. I could not stay on the streets.

SPORK, punkbunnypopsicle, punkbunnypopsicle, im lonely, no one loves me

Daddy! NO one LOVES ME!!!" The Wiseman says, "You must take revenge on them...using the power of the Dark Crystal!" Suddenly, the black rings enclose on her. ...

I want a family, I want friends, I want everything that I don't have, I am a blue Elephante, I am blue because I am sad, No one loves me.

You have Chocobo Ghost to love you! (looks all innocent and hurt) Unlike me...no-one loves me...

And I want your input on this one, too ... PWEASE? SORRY! Whatever, NO one loves me ...? but some nectarine out there loves this lonely tangerine ... tee, hee!

I am going talk about how no one loves me until the words feel fake in my mouth.

THE VICTORY OF FOLLY (AS PLUTO)

My Victory makes noise that goes thud thud thud thud.

Is My Victory Normal?

What's Up With My Victory?

What's the tiny red bump on my victory?

"Look at my victory and fear me"

Oh dear. At least, they never said anything, and they all seemed to like my victory.

Why has my victory lost sensitivity?

Sounds of My Victory

When I try to masturbate a small amount of white lubricant comes out from the middle of my victory.

What is priapism? Whom should I thank for my victory?

You can basically pull it out of my victory, almost like a noodle.

On the underside of my victory, there is a fairly large, bluish-purplish vein that branches out.

She then continued the gender-bending and named my victory "Stephanie."

What the hell, a chipmunk just bit my victory.

The hair on my Victory.

MY VICTORY IS IN YOUR BUTT

My dog recently passed away.

I had a dog, now I only have my victory.

PORPO-THANG

The porpoises fling up their
orange underthings; swaying
in the wind, their heavy rotation
is brief and horrifying,

full of bright scrawls, of thin
and lacy garters.
There isn't a place
in this world that doesn't

sooner or later drown
in the porridge of upload,
but now, for a while,
the bustier

shines like an undertaker
as it floats above everything
with its yellow cognitive science.
Of course nothing stops the flimsy,

black, curved porousness
from bending forward—
of course
restlessness is the great undertone.

But I also say this: that thongs
are an invitation
to undervaluation,
and that undervaluation,

when it's done right,
is a kind of porousness,
palpitating and porphyritic.
Inside the tight fields,

touched by their rough and spongy noises,
I am washed and washed
in the porridge
of satin delight—

and what are you going to do—
what *can* you do
about it—
flung, orange negligee?

SHE SURE LIKES THE CREAM

(song version: to the tune of "De Temps en Temps")

O pussycat
O fluffy kitten
She's a furry semiotic machine
a rabid glass-eyed princess
With her cunning kitty dreams

O dreamy girl
O moody sweetie
Like the man who would be queen
pussycat don't like the soup but
she sure likes the cream

She believes our anxieties
are like cunnilingus
or like electric ferrets
Darling little catheads
With pretty little bows

Moonshine lady sugar
and blue bubbles
A belabored metaphor in pantyhose!

O pussycat
O fluffy kitten
She's an animal mujahedeen
a one-eyed voodoo goddess
With a clashing color scheme

O dreamy girl
O moody sweetie
She's a feline wolverine
pussycat don't like the soup but
she sure likes the cream

She believes our society
should be iridescent
like chaotic parrots
Darling little rabbits
In simulated mind

Moonshine lady sugar
and blue bubbles
She's the emblem of a culture in decline!

lalala section
(ending with)
pussycat don't like the soup but
She sure likes the cream

SANDRA LIM

VEXED PRESSED FROCK

around the ill na na we played jacks. hopscotch. swilled it to the tick-tack-toe. little cosmonauts, blooming super-fools. crowing "ill na na" in the marmalade. told it fortunes, explained the circulatory system. sassed it, na na, cheered madly madly. gamely irritable, adorable. indolent and homemade. country mouse meet city mouse. so glad like a birthday cake, ill na na.

GIVE ME BACK THE OLD WRONG THING

My blush.   I came out of some goblinry,
a blubber of oboes announced this.
There is no question   it's terrestrial &
ensnared in tendrils,   up to something.
Minimum   shebang. Like hearing a wall.
Love, lie by the personal   survive my
inquisitorial crawl.   Bell boldly the advance:
say Bully for you   & for me.
I am a creeper under   merry leaves
touching poignantly, vexing so.
These days I lost my mind.   One tree each.
Belle day   flaps closed. I peaked for a night-
bird plea, the quavers of it   lapping.
Envious of its blue will   & unkeyed
pining sweet, selfsame.   Silvered, I was salt
& groveling   shook from heat. I
am no kindness   & no truthful
recall. No demoiselle.   The most I can say
love, is that I toss   centerless.
When the clouds free I am tempted to say,
There was no such thing!   I am lost!
& bear me away.

MEASURE

Girls
          For the lowing of whales
has conjured them up   given them savage details,
cut off their braids.   Seahorses ride their eyes
out. I am one of those   with a dimple in the mind.
A gleam in the foam   astral, tonight. Don't ruin
them with—   don't wake them, the warm
anemones deflate it.   Failing sun, go after
sand, all thousand bits.   Ocean me, be larger than
promise. Eased into skirt.   Talk not of mermaids.

Whales
          The vaulting green and drift
of that day   white distances opened, run high.
Blue proceeds   —like bones, like time— to
its designated junctures,   tremendous as girls.

IT INCREASED US

They would chew the insides of their mouths out
& spit them at you. One day
it's all pinky promises, rhinestone tiaras &
eating hot French fries at midnight.
Tender mooing & then,
something is tearing a hole into the air.
They appeared smooth as pancakes once,
now they throw a shadow. I love:
the soft malice in the way that they
surge into themselves, bleeding
smoke from their fingertips.
Cute to acute, & then, & then—

SARAH VAP

SURLY PIGGIES

Luckily-cripplingly— let's highlight my well-being
for a moment: this little self-actualized life-long friend.

This pretty baby unicorn

tucks me in. This shabby workhorse
breaks a promise.   This little workforce waits for father's wink—it is a
penance—

this hankered after pays its own way.
This little potency   shares as much benevolence with the world
as she can. This "No-fault" divorce
unites my theory

with practice.   For partnerships out of love's reach. This little prophecy—what the
New
Masculinity should flush: this, strictly speaking, *wee wee wee*

through the church-contest.   To the junctures of my meta-
tarsals   (I jokingly call "the wimps"). Or, my brave little

uprights.

LITTLE GIRLS AND HORSES

In the burning grapefruit grove you decide never again to speak
with someone you love. Because they're dragging. Or, as I like to say,
your money where your mouth is loosey-goosey. Flawed and wonderful,
asking repeatedly: So many thousands of offerings? Bullshit
you're not looking at that willow tree, I said—and vice-versa. Like some old
horse-mentor, careful to be extra-respectful because he was strange enough
to square away a table. And you'll do it too—selling and breeding
as lovers and judges—and as a teasing bounce—
why to me right now you're so short-lived. Why you're slipping through
the window to the mercies of the world.

EVENTIDE

Unbearable dress—do you have a secret
memory of a cow

tormented by the gadfly. *What the fuck is the gadfly?*

Unaccountable—why there's a planetarium in the Nebraska
cornfield. Io is the closest
of Jupiter's moons. Galileo

found the cashcow first. Tart. Flippant. Cowgirl-magnificat
in the vulnerable dress.

LITTLE CLOUDS ON TEETH

Terrible, how we stare at the man's
delicate ankles—as we imagine Jesus's feet. You qualify the feet by saying

they don't fit. Sorry because cat's-eye is heavy-lidded,
partway open—don't believe everything you read, Chicken. Twins are examples
of clones, and both taste like chicken.

Light-brown river—something aluminum
in the palm-tree, like a pink chicken in the monsoon. Like Sarah Bernhardt
as Hamlet, believing everything she reads. Wind blows the tears

right out of her eyes—the curtain
embroidered with reverential cattails.

A WINDOW THE SIZE OF A GRANNY'S FOREHEAD

1.
Through which can be seen
a star, blades of grass.

Grocery receipts
between panes. Crying,

but crying out—the woman-hen

who didn't last and the white
flies around her. The grannies

in the sky—does this one have
a home anywhere, or is she

perhaps a found behemoth angel.

2.
Come, come
Granny—the boat

underwater with stained glass.

Granny bombing
so everything will turn

to glass. Summer
and winter gods drown

together. Parachutes of light—

the need
for anyone to last.

3.
But not to act. Granny pulls
single hairs

from the sky. Tells

who has been quiet. Who took
to her knowing

and the melting,
correct. Granny horsing.

4.
Granny, Granny, calm down.
Who thinks

of you smoothing

your clay shawl. Your glass
daughter and a line

of hens in sky.

HALLOWEEN POEM

I'm going as ballast. Last year you were the shoreline
wrapped in plastic.　　　Promise this—

let's go as the heartwarming gag to sell and scare and flourish the little pink dog.
Let's go as a hot-pink dot—and three-part Boo. Go! You, be a bag

inside a wife. (To steady the vessel—

how many elves fit inside.) In a manner of speaking—if you work hard
you'll succeed with a bag of candy—

but notice a couple things

they didn't say before… why they're doing what they're doing about
the treats. Who they choose

to suspect, and why. Realistically, it just seems right where faith

and tricking collide with the classic

losing manhood—like a puppy. And consequentially—
we'll go as approaching the other cheek

with total enthusiasm and the hissy-fit.

STACY DORIS

FIRST HOME MOVIE TRIPTYCH, IN KORANIC* ORDER
*(going from longest to shortest parts)

ACTION:

I

From under a shower of pinkest rose petals, from a green runway scattered with melancholy Roman ruins, from behind the palace's heavy crimson tapestries COME, *crawling on all fours, again, a pack of (debauched) kings and queens*, heavily panting through their soused maws. Reaching the imperial beds, they climb up and sink into a stupor. Bubbles of champagne trickle between snores from their senseless mouths. The crowns tilt ridiculously atop their slipping wigs. Only one queen, insatiable, is kept awake by her sadistic lust. She pushes aside the royal corpses, ferreting her way out to the corridor where a bevy of stripped milkmaids, starving and half-frozen from their wait in the drafty hall, lip-synching the words to *The Farmer in the Dell*, are instructed to "milk" the queen, who, mooing on her hands and knees, climaxes an average of three times a minute from this abuse. Finally, her thirst momentarily abated, she struggles to her feet and, wielding an enormous whip, punishes the maidens until the walls and floor are red with their virginal blood. They fall down the long marble staircase, their disgrace exposed to the eyes of impassive guards in full military dress. *The Farmer in the Dell* record skips.

DUMB FASHION SHOW
(IN THE COUR CARRÉE OF THE LOUVRE)
(A NEWSREEL TRIPTYCH)

Part One: BACKSTAGE

*Six hairdressers, on ladders, armed with hairpicks, gels, and sprays, tease the tresses of a marquise up to ceiling height. Marquise, careful not to so much as blink, rotates her eyeballs in their sockets, her only recourse to expression. A sudden gale rattles the window. An ember falls from the chandelier onto the marquise's (*MARQUISE *"A"*) *bouffant, and—poof—she's burnt to a crisp. Hairdressers, diving from the wreck of their flaming ladders, sob uncontrollably.*

Part Two: ON THE RUNWAY

An assortment of MARQUISES, DUCHESSES, *and* DAMES *pull up in a line of closed ceremonial carriages with holes sawed in the roofs from which their hairdos massively protrude. They are delicately extracted and led to the team of* COIFFEURS *for last-minute touch-ups. Finally, glued, bulwarked and plumped, they form a line and parade in the following order (each bearing the name of her coiffure on a placard):*

Cleopatra

Candor

Sentimental Journey

Fields in Time of Harvest

Royal Pheasant Hunt

Disaster at Sea

Cupid and Psyche

The Silly Goose

The Ugly Duckling

Map of the World

Iphigenia

Small Pox Inoculation (or, The Death of Louis XV)

Marriage of Figaro

Puss in Boots

~~Declaration of Independence at Philadelphia~~

Slaying of the First Born

The Hangman (or The Executioner Sanson)

Sweet Temptation

Cookies and Cream

A crowd of the Panty-Less (Sans-Culottes) press against the barricades, hurl-ing tarts, vegetables, and pebbles which lodge in the vast clouds of hair, brightening the color scheme without essentially perturbing the impassive serenity of the high-born models' heads.

Part Three: THE PENCHANT FOR FEATHERS;,
            or, RECIPE FOR THE REDISTRIBUTION OF WEALTH

MORNING. HER MAJESTY, *awakening, is brought a breast-shaped bowl of hot chocolate and the Grande (Larousse) Encyclopedie de la FRIVOLITÉ from which she is meant to choose the day's foibles. She opens, at random, to p. 600 and reads:*

THE PENCHANT FOR FEATHERS: Basic Instructions:
Enter, with light skipping steps, *lestement*, graceful lady (Her Majesty as YOUNG DAUPHINE?), fully stripped, pregnant, bobbing; her face hidden behind a huge headdress in the form of a rutting male peacock. Spreading her arms wide, with neck and torso undulating in imitation of a strutting fowl, she moves in a circle round and round the naked, kneeling, wildly aroused M. PEXTO (or PEIXTO?), the tailor. Presently, heeding the tailor's gruff command, lady crouches to straddle him from behind. "My fine bird," the tailor murmurs repeatedly, upon which signal the (DAUPHINE) extracts a feather from her headdress and tickles herself with it briefly before planting it in M. PEXTO's (or PEIXTO?)'s uplifted anus.

Continue until all of the feathers have been transferred.

CLASSIFIEDS:

UP FOR AUCTION: Cosmetic Kit of Mme the Duchesse Sourde, including, in addition to all the usual accessories (false teeth, false braids, false lashes, falsies) a false mount of Venus, hand-crafted by the Queen's hairdresser, for the exclusive use of Monsieur, His Former Majesty the King's great uncle.

FOR SALE: Charming bronze statuette having belonged to the Countess Polignac, composed of a woman's head, sphinx's breasts, eagle claws, and the tail of a pig. Suitable for insertion in a variety of orifices.

LOST: One Flame-red muff of royal fox, belonging to Her Former Majesty, who can't remember where she last left it, nor what was stuffed inside it at the time. Fearing that this muff might go to ruin if unattended, Her Former Majesty offers an indulgent reward to whoever finds it.

WANTED: DEAD OR ALIVE: *WARNING*: a female panther, brought to our fair city from an Austrian menagerie, after living peacefully in the Royal Zoo for a number of years, is thought to have escaped. Last spotted in the company of a rabid she-wolf. This wild beast is strong, powerful, inflamed, and red in color. A reward of 20,000 is offered in return for information leading to her capture.

SITUATION WANTED: Cokie, darling cocker spaniel pup to the former Royal Governess, and until recently in highest favor with the mistress in question, finding himself replaced by General Mortier (Lafayette), seeks new lady. Willing to fill all positions.

FOR SALE TO THE HIGHEST BIDDER: Pretty shell-shaped bathtub, 100% pure marble inside and out, ideally suited for early morning blood baths, from the former quarters of the former King's spinster aunts, Mesdames Adéläde, Victoire, and Sophie. Comfortably accommodates three to five bathers.

SPECIAL OFFER: Act now to receive a bonus gift box of human skulls straight from the former Royal Nursery, perfect for the serving of Royal Porridge *à volon-*

té (all you can eat).

<u>MISCELLANEOUS</u>: From the former Versailles apothecary: Set of syringes, equipped with needles, suitable for poisoning friends and family, political figures and nobility alike (Mauperas, Mirabeau, Mlle d'Oliva, etc.). Plus, at no additional cost, a copy (facsimile) of the recipe book containing Marie de Médicis' favorite, fool-proof concoctions.

<u>TO ORDER</u>: 'Flayed Minstrel' figurines, made from you choice of human, kitten, or monkey fetuses, in the tradition of the anatomical genius Fragonard. These are faithful reproductions of pieces found missing from the curiosity cabinet of the former Louis XV.

TINA BROWN CELONA

SUNDAY MORNING CUNT POEM

I wrote a book of contiguous poems then mixed them up so they were out of order. They were poems about my cunt, language, Nature, war, and all of them had a marked sense of drama.

With the cunt poems I could have orgasms during sex. I had long, luxurious hair, which I wrapped around my throat like a scarf. You could say I was "released from my prison." My therapist was no longer busy.

We started a business called Ethical Donuts. It was actually a kind of juice bar where you could go and read poems or listen to someone reading poems. If nobody felt like reading poems we would turn on a tape of someone reading poems, usually one of our friends, but sometimes a big star of poetry. Of course, we sold donuts.

In my dream we were hitchhiking to Iowa City, but later when I looked at myself my cheeks were pink and so were my labia. Like a bird I discovered I had wings. I flew higher and higher, but when I got near the sun the wax melted and I fell into a poem by Auden. It was then that I wrote the poem "The Enormous Cock."

For awhile I hushed. Then I started up again about my cunt. Some said it was a vicious swipe at feminism. Others said it was a vicious feminist swipe. It was the only word I knew.

I THREW AWAY MY GUN AND MY HARNESS

I threw away my gun and my harness. I was no longer a superhero. Imagine this most ideal of situations: one's eye is forever lighting on beautiful things, one's emotions are aroused, one's hand expresses these emotions through the pen, which sentiments are interpreted by another, causing (in this most ideal of scenarios) the other to feel and see. Imagine this glorious image blotted out by a sinister black cloud. Imagine the cloud leaking and the drops spattering and diving among the flowers. When will men stop desiring young girls? He goes to work early wearing his most handsome shirt.

For an hour I take pictures of my cunt. Spread cunt, panties pulled askew, prim virginal cunt, cunt with asshole, cunt without asshole. I make a photo album, one cunt on each page.

I never wrote the ending of this poem. You are not reading it now.

POEM FOR GIRLS

1.

You can read all about yourself in this poem
And that's why it's fun.
Everyone wants to be in this poem
But this poem is only for girls.

2.

In spring the barberry leaves are lettuce-red.
In fall they are the color of the sun
As it explodes.
The willows leaf out
Long before the oaks.
You're thinking about your computer as a girl
And I'm jealous.
I think, "It doesn't make me want to quote it,"
And then I think "happy disco-colored elephants."

3.

There is always a more
Truthful truth. Sensitive, beautiful emotions
Swirl around me like snowflakes.
I look at the cat.
One of us has farted.

EVENT DIARY

That evening I am thrilled to discover I am still alive. I breathe and it makes a whistling sound. I gnash my teeth and make Dracula faces and stay outside in the car until it is too late.

When I finally do it I realize I have been putting it off all day. The polar bear tipped me off but I was still surprised when I woke up this morning with a rubber heart.

The elements of our day were as follows: church, graveyard, community garden, Luna Park, museum park, museum, car, Golden Gate Park, bar, reading, car. I reach for my coffee nastily as a dumbbell nebula fizzes in the distance.

Is there any more?

Naturally there is, there's John Godfrey. He's come all the way from Brooklyn and Bill Berkson, Leslie Scalapino and Kevin Killian are in the audience. Bill and Kevin ignore me but Leslie says hi.

There's a field full of nasturtiums and a ratty columbine and the headlight crashes down the trash chute to land in a quivering pile of filaments and Tic Tacs. I light a little pyre in the yard and wander around aimlessly thinking about things. Then I realize the things are actually thinking about me.

DINKY LOGIC

I was ill from the mental rays. They shot them with their eyes. People who matter never notice when you compliment them on their glasses. Or on their parrot.

I moved to a safer place away from the mental rays. I bent my eyes down. They did not want me to help with their party.

As the mountain lion explained, he did not get along with the other mountain lions. He would get along with the ewes because they liked the shape of his groin. But he was not a favorite among the mountain lions.

SPRING IN PARIS

for Justine

The wind in my bikini
is not in my bikini after all.
It lurks in the strings
And in the soft flap
Between my legs,
and it is waving like a flag
on the raft of the Medusa
in the Louvre in Paris
or wherever the Louvre may be now.

By the fur of Maurice the dog I love you.

I admit the sand of the rooftop, the fish of the friary,
the eggs of the amoeba, the beak of the apothecary.

You do not think of me
now. Your husband would be
more likely to think of me:
catastrophe.

By the last drop of wine
in the smallest glass I beseech you

By the yellow fuzz
on the banana slug

I entreat you.

How can I tell him that everything
is useless without you
to hear, you
with your cultivated ear.

LAUGHING MAN (*excerpt from* "**POEM FOR MATT**")

It was when my brain started showing its teeth to people that I became LAUGH-ING MAN. Fluffs and fluffs of poetry were in my hands, it was like being in a cloud. My hair peeled back and there were the teeth all exposed in a row like a dog's jaw. Everyone clapped!!! But it was as if my brain had clamped down on the dog's leash and run off trailing the happy crowd.
I had never had my brain in my stomach before!!

Just leave me alone with the girl in the casserole, I'm licking her incredible neck, and get those laughing, tuxedo-clad, mermaid-tailed lobster claws out of the pic-ture. God damn it,

Let's start over. I need a pair of pants to go with my shirt, I need a pair of boots to go with my hat, I wish I lived in a factory where you had everything you need-ed to make anything you wanted.

Poets

Ariana Reines was born in 1980 in Salem, Massachusetts. She is the author of *The Cow* (2006 Alberta Prize, FenceBooks) and *Coeur de Lion* (Mal-o-Mar 2007). TELEPHONE, her first play, was commissioned by The Foundry Theatre and produced in February 2009 at The Cherry Lane Theatre in New York. *My Heart Laid Bare*, a translation of Baudelaire, for Mal-O-Mar, and a translation of works by Grisélidis Réal, for Semiotext(e), will also appear in 2009.

Arielle Greenberg was born in 1972, and her books include *My Kafka Century* (Action, 2005) and *Given* (Verse/Wave, 2002), the chapbook *Far(t)her Down: Song from the Allergy Trials* (New Michigan, 2003), and, with Rachel Zucker, *Women Poets on Mentorship: Efforts & Affections* (Iowa, 2008). She came up with the theory of the Gurlesque in 2000. As a young girl she loved unicorns, sorrowful acoustic music, glitter, the counterculture, snow-globes, dollhouses, Playboy, vintage clothing, and baby animals, and she still loves all these same things. In the early 90s she published a pop culture/feminist/riot grrl zine called *William Wants a Doll* whose archives are now housed as part of the zine collection at the Sallie Bingham Center for Women's History and Culture at the Duke University Rare Book, Manuscript and Special Collections Library. She lives with a daughter, a son, a man, and a dog, and is an associate professor at Columbia College Chicago.

Brenda Coultas was born in 1958 in Owensboro, Kentucky, grew up in Southern Indiana, graduated from the Naropa Institute in 1994 where she studied under Allen Ginsberg and Anne Waldman, and moved to the Lower East Side in 1995 to work at the Poetry Project in St. Marks Church in the Bowerie. She is the author of *A Handmade Museum* (Coffee House, 2003), which won the Norma Farber Award from The Poetry Society of America, and a Greenwall Fund publishing grant from the Academy of American Poets. She has served as program assistant, newsletter editor, series curator and teacher at the Poetry Project in NYC. Her writing can be found in many publications including *Conjunctions*, *Explosive*, *Brooklyn Rail* and *Bombay Gin*. Other books include *Early Films* (Rodent Press) and *A Summer Newsreel* (Second Story Press). She has lived a block from the Bowery for the past ten years.

Brenda Shaughnessy was born in Okinawa, Japan, and raised in Southern California. She is the author of *Interior with Sudden Joy* and *Human Dark with Sugar* (Copper Canyon Press 2008), which won the 2007 James Laughlin Award, and was a finalist for the 2008 National Book Critics Circle Award. Her poems have been published in *Bomb*, *Conjunctions*, *McSweeney's*, *The New Yorker*, *The Paris Review*, *The Yale Review*, and elsewhere. She is the Poetry Editor of *Tin House Magazine* and and is currently Lecturer in Poetry at Princeton University and Writer in Residence at Eugene Lang College at the New School. She lives in Brooklyn with her husband and son.

Catherine Wagner was born in Burma in 1969 and grew up in Baltimore. She is the author of three books from Fence: *My New Job* (2009), *Macular Hole* (2004) and *Miss America* (2001). Recent chapbooks include *Articulate How* (Big Game/Dusie, 2009), *Everyone in the Room is a Representative of the World at Large* (Bonfire, 2007) and *Hole in the Ground* (Slack Buddha, 2008). She teaches poetry at Miami University in Oxford, Ohio.

Cathy Park Hong was born in 1976 in Los Angeles. Her first book, *Translating Mo'um*, was published in 2002 by Hanging Loose Press. Her second collection, *Dance Dance Revolution*, was chosen for the Barnard Women Poets Prize and was published in 2007 by WW Norton. Hong is also the recipient of a Fulbright Fellowship and National Endowment for the Arts Fellowship. Her poems have been published in *A Public Space*, *American Letters & Commentary*, *Denver Quarterly*, *Verse*, *Chain*, *Jubilat*, and other journals, and she has reported for the *Village Voice*, *The Guardian*, and *Salon*. She teaches at Sarah Lawrence College.

Chelsey Minnis was born in 1970. She is not a born native of Colorado but has lived there for much of her life and attended the University of Colorado at Boulder. She also attended the Iowa Writer's Workshop in poetry. Her first book, *Zirconia*, won the Alberta Prize for Women from Fence Press in 2001. Fence Books published her second manuscript *Bad Bad* in 2007. Her third book, *Poemland*, is scheduled be published by Wave Books in 2009.

Danielle Pafunda was born in 1977. She is author of *Iatrogenic: Their Testimonies* (Noemi Press forthcoming), *My Zorba* (Bloof Books 2008), *Pretty Young Thing* (Soft Skull Press 2005), and the forthcoming *Manhater* (Dusie Press). For seven years she was editor of *La Petite Zine*, and now curates poetics forums at *Delirious Hem*. She teaches gender studies, English literature, and creative writing at the University of Wyoming, and lives on the frontier with partner and charges.

Dorothea Lasky is the author of *AWE* (Wave Books, 2007) and *Black Life* (Wave Books, 2010). Her poems have appeared in *American Poetry Review*, *Boston Review*, *Columbia Poetry Review*, *The Laurel Review*, *The New Yorker*, *The Paris Review*, and *Satellite Telephone*, among other places. She's been educated at Harvard University, University of Massachusetts-Amherst, and Washington University. Currently, she researches creativity and education at the University of Pennsylvania. Videos of her reading her poems along with other poets can be found on www.birdinsnow.com.

Elizabeth Treadwell was born in Oakland, California on the cusp of the so-called summer of love (1967) and grew mainly up in the wilds of Berkeley. She worked in Hollywood briefly, and ran Small Press Traffic in San Francisco during a smidge of Clinton and most of Bush 2. She's the author of a novel, a collection of stories and prose poems, six assorted chapbooks, and five books of poetry, including her most recent, *Wardolly* (2008).

Geraldine Kim was born in 1983 with six nipples: two primary nipples, two sub nipples above the primary nipples, and two nipples close to her armpits. They each have an eerie symmetry with the other breast, which further creeps out gynecologists, women in the locker room, and people she has slept with. She has only slept with four people in her entire life so she isn't a whore and even if she was why is having sex with a lot of people a bad thing? Anyway, she's really insecure about her nipples so don't ask her about it (them?).

Heidi Lynn Staples is the author of *Guess Can Gallop* (New Issues 2004) and *Dog Girl* (Ahsahta 2007), and she's the mother of Sophie Karen Staples. Most every day the two stroll to pat the cherry trees and say hello. They gather fallen petals. They peek between fence rails at pansies. Heidi Lynn Staples says, Oh isn't that pretty?! And Sophie Karen Staples says Mmmm Hmmmm!. They stow hydrangea in their buttonholes and sweetpea blossoms behind their ears and heather in their pockets. They pluck clover flower and puff dandelions and gather roses from their own garden into bouquets which fill their house with perfume. O what a gender-inflected preoccupation! O what an unqualified fixation on the soft and the delicate! O so many dialects of pink!

Kim Rosenfield was born in 1966. She is the author of three books of poetry: *Good Morning—Midnight—* (Roof Books 2001), which won Small Press Traffic's Book of the Year award in 2002; *Tràma* (Krupskaya 2004); and *re: evolution* (forthcoming from Les Figues Press in 2008). She lives in NYC with her husband, poet Robert Fitterman, and their daughter, Coco.

Lara Glenum is a linguistic ruse perpetrated by a salacious group of horse skeletons. She has routinely been sighted by ornithologists since 1970. Books commonly attributed to her include: *The Hounds of No* (Action Books, 2005) and *Maximum Gaga* (Action Books, 2008). Alleged activities include occult proselytizing in a Louisiana swamp (LSU) and travels to Prague to engage in acts of avant-garde translation. Criminologists have also linked her to the multimedia art cell that produced *Meat Out of the Eater* and other such disreputable flimflam.

Matthea Harvey was born in Bad Homburg, Germany in 1973. She is the author of three books of poetry: *Modern Life* (Graywolf, 2007), a finalist for the National Book Critics Circle Award, *Sad Little Breathing Machine* (Graywolf, 2004), *Pity the Bathtub Its Forced Embrace of the Human Form* (Alice James Books, 2000), and a children's book titled *The Little General and the Giant Snowflake*. She teaches poetry at Sarah Lawerence and lives in Brooklyn. Her website is http://www.mattheaharvey.info.

Nada Gordon was born in 1964 and, as a child, sang on a song called "Free Rain" released on the Jefferson Airplane's Grunt label by the band One, whose lead singer was Reality D. Blipcrotch. She became a hardcore punk rocker at 14, and in 1988 moved to Tokyo, where she lived for eleven years. Nada is the author of four poetry books: *Folly* (Roof Books), *V. Imp*, *Are Not Our Lowing Heifers Sleeker than Night-Swollen Mushrooms?*, *foriegnn bodie* and, with Gary Sullivan, an epistolary techno-romantic non-fiction novel, *Swoon*. She practices poetry as deep entertainment and is a proud member of the Flarflist Collective. Visit her blog at http://ululate.blogspot.com.

Sandra Lim is the author of *Loveliest Grotesque* (Kore Press, 2006). She was born in Seoul, Korea in 1973 and grew up in California. She received her B.A. from Stanford, her Ph.D. from U.C. Berkeley, and her M.F.A. from the Iowa Writers' Workshop. Her work has appeared in *American Letters & Commentary*, *Denver Quarterly*, *Boston Review*, *Colorado Review*, and other journals. Currently, she is a visiting poet-in-residence at Columbia College of Chicago..

Sarah Vap is the author of *American Spikenard*, winner of the 2006 Iowa Poetry Prize, and *Dummy Fire*, winner of the 2006 Saturnalia Poetry Prize. She was born in Wichita, Kansas in 1972, and grew up in Missoula, Montana. Vap spent the 70's and 80's swimming, riding horses and pretending to be a member of the Lewis and Clark Expedition. She attended Brown University, then the Arizona State University MFA program. She currently lives on the Olympic Peninsula with her partner, Todd Fredson, their two sons, and an almost-40-year-old horse. Her third collection, *Faulkner's Rosary*, is forthcoming from Saturnalia Books.

Stacy Doris was born in 1962. Her books written in English include *Cheerleader's Guide to the World: Council Book*, *Knot*, *Conference*, *Paramour* and *Kildare*. Forthcoming from Jank is *The Cake Part*, from which the poems in this anthology are taken. Written in French are *Parlement* and, semi-anonymously, *La vie de Chester Steven Wiener écrite par sa femme*, and *Une année à New York avec Chester*. She has co-edited three collections of French poetry translated by American poets, among them, with Chet Wiener, *Christophe Tarkos: Ma Langue est Poétique--Selected Work*. She is currently working on several audio commissions, including a commission to record eighteenth-century perfumes with co-poet Lisa Robertson.

Tina Brown Celona was born in 1974. She is the author of a chapbook, *Songs and Scores*, (Spectacular Books, 1999) and two books, *The Real Moon of Poetry and Other Poems* (Fence Books, 2002) and *Snip Snip!* (Fence Books, 2006). She is currently a Ph.D. candidate at the University of Denver.

Visual Artists

Alessandra Exposito was born in 1970. She received her MFA from the Mason Gross School of the Arts at Rutgers in 1998 and has shown in numerous group exhibitions in New York City and beyond. Venues include the Academy of Arts and Letters (NY, NY), the Nathan Cummings Foundation (NY, NY), The Shore Institute of Contemporary Arts (Long Branch, NJ) and Art in General (NY, NY). Museum exhibitions include "Open House, Working in Brooklyn," at the Brooklyn Museum of Art and "El Museo's Biennial" at El Museo del Barrio, New York. She was the recipient of a MacDowell Colony residence and in 2005 won the Richard and Hinda Rosenthal Foundation Award and the Purchase Award from the American Academy of Arts and Letters. In 2007, she won a New York Foundation for the Arts fellowship in sculpture.

Audrey Kawasaki was born in 1982. She studied painting at the Pratt Institute, and has had work featured in exhibitions in Tokyo (Space Yui), Rome (Mondo Bizarro), and Los Angeles (Thinkspace Gallery) and has a solo show at the Jonathan Levine Gallery in New York City in 2009.

Dame Darcy was born in 1971. She attended the San Francisco Art Institute, where she studied with George Kuchar, Kathy Acker, and others. During this time Dame Darcy began self-publishing her long standing comic book *Meat Cake*, currently published by Fantagraphics Books and on its 16th issue and counting. She also performs in several bands (and plays banjo, bass, and singing saw), makes short films, and produced the show Turn Of the Century, which ran for four years on Manhattan Public access. She has released the graphic novels *The Illustrated Jane Eyre* (Putnam Penguin), *Frightful Fairytales* (Ten Speed Press), *Dame Darcy's Meat Cake Compilation* (Fantagraphics Books) and several musical recordings.

E.V. Day was born in 1967. Her work is in the permanent collections of the Museum of Modern Art in New York, the National Museum of Women in the Arts in Washington, D.C., the San Francisco Museum of Modern Art and the Saatchi Collection in London, among others, and has been shown in solo exhibitions at Deitch Projects in New York, the Indianapolis Museum of Art, the Herbert F. Johnson Museum of Art at Cornell University and the Whitney Museum of American Art at Philip Morris in New York. She was a 2007 New York Foundation for the Arts sculpture fellow and has an MFA in sculpture from Yale.

Hope Atherton was born in 1974. She has a BFA from the Rhode Island School of Design. Her work has been shown at Patrick Painter in Los Angeles, P.S. 1 Contemporary Art Center in New York, and Galleria Gian Enzo Sperone in Rome.

Kara Walker was born in 1969. She received her BFA from the Atlanta College of Art and her MFA from the Rhode Island School of Design. She was included in the 1997 Biennial exhibition at the Whitney Museum of American Art, New York. Later that year, at the age of 27, she became the youngest recipient of the prestigious John D. and Catherine T. MacArthur Foundation's "genius" grant, and in 2002 she was chosen to represent the United States in the São Paulo Biennial in Brazil. Her work has been exhibited nationally and internationally and is included in the collections of major museums worldwide. The 2007 Walker Art Center–organized exhibition *Kara Walker: My Complement, My Oppressor, My Enemy, My Love* was her first full-scale U.S. museum survey. She is a professor of visual arts in the MFA program at Columbia University.

Lady Aiko (AKA Aiko Nakagawa) was born in 1975. She is one of the founding members of Faile, an international street art collective. She has had work shown at the Brooklyn Museum, the Joshua Liner Gallery in New York, New Image Art in Los Angeles, Art Basel Miami, Revelations in Tokyo, and elsewhere, and Kid Robot produced a limited edition vinyl figure of her Aiko Bunny in 2008.

Lauren Kalman was born in 1980. She has an MFA in Art from the Ohio State University and a BFA, with a focus in metals, from Massachusetts College of Art. Her solo exhibitions include the Cheekwood Museum of Art in Nashville and the Sculpture Center in Cleveland and her professional experience includes employment at the Johnson Atelier Technical Institute of Sculpture and the New Jersey State Council on the Arts. Her work is in the permanent collection of the Museum of Fine Arts, Boston. She is currently a part-time professor at Brown University.

PERMISSIONS

Poets

ARIANA REINES "Documentary Poetry," "Blowhole," "Knocker," I Love My Emergency," "And Blindly We Forefeel," "Anthem," "Fated," "Earmark," "Valve" copyright 2006 © by the author. Originally appeared in *The Cow* published by Fence Books in 2006. Reprinted by permission of the author and publisher. "from *Couer de Lion*" copyright 2007 © by the author. Originally appeared in *Couer de Lion* published by Mal-o-Mar Editions in 2007. Reprinted by permission of the author. "In the Evening Tozan Swam..." originally appeared in *Soft Targets* 2.1 in 2007. Reprinted by permission of the author.

BRENDA COULTAS "dream life in a case of transvestism" and "margaret" copyright 1996 © by the author. Originally appeared in *Early Films* published by Rodent Press in 1996. Reprinted by permission of the author. "II" copyright 1999 © by the author. Originally appeared in *A Summer Newsreel* published by Second Story Books in 1999. Reprinted by permission of the author. "The Shed" from The Marvelous Bones of Time: Excavations and Explanations. Copyright © 2007 by Brenda Coultas. Reprinted with the permission of Coffee House Press, Minneapolis, Minnesota, www.coffeehousepress.org.

BRENDA SHAUGHNESSY "Dear Gongyla," "Your One Good Dress," and "Arachnolescence" from *Interior with Sudden Joy* by Brenda Shaughnessy. Copyright © 1999 by Brenda Shaughnessy. Reprinted by permission of Farrar, Straus and Giroux, LLC. "Parthenogenesis" and "First Date and Still Very, Very Lonely," "I'm Over the Moon," from *Human Dark with Sugar*. Copyright " 2008 by Brenda Shaughnessy. Reprinted with the permission of Copper Canyon Press, www.coppercanyonpress.org.

CATHERINE WAGNER "All Bar One," "Café Rouge," "White Man Poems," copyright 2001 © by the author, from *Miss America*, published by Fence Books in 2001 (first published in the chapbook *Hotel Faust*, West House Books, England, 2001). Reprinted by permission of the author and publisher. "I soaped myself " and "My greed was outrageous," from "Imitating," copyright 2004 © by the author, from *Macular Hole*, published by Fence Books in 2004 (first published in the chapbook *Imitating*, Leafe Press, England, 2004). Reprinted by permission of the author and publisher. "The Argument," "This Is a Fucking Poem," "Coming and I Did Not Run Away" and "For the boys," copyright 2009 © by the author, from *My New Job*, published by Fence Books in 2009 (first published in the chapbook *Hole in the Ground*, Slack Buddha, 2008). Reprinted by permission of the author and publisher.

CATHY PARK HONG "Rite of Passage," "All the Aphrodisiacs," "On Splitting," "Zoo," copyright 2002 © by the author. Originally appeared in *Translating Mo'um* published by Hanging Loose Press in 2002. Reprinted by permission of the author and publisher. "The Hoola Hoopers' Taunt," "Karaoke Lounge," "Almanac," from Dance Dance Revolution by Cathy Park Hong. Copyright 2007 © by Cathy Park Hong. Used by permission of W. W. Norton & Company.

CHELSEY MINNIS "Uh," "Sectional," "Primrose," copyright 2001 © by the author. Originally appeared in *Zirconia* published by Fence Books in 2001. "Preface 1," "Preface 13," "Fifi No, No," copyright 2007 © by the author. Originally appeared in *Bad Bad* published by Fence Books in 2007. Reprinted by permission of the author and publisher. "tiger d" and "wench" copyright 2009 © by the author. Reprinted by permission of the author.

Also Available from **saturnalia books**:

Personification by Margaret Ronda
Winner of the Saturnalia Books Poetry Prize 2009

Tsim Tsum by Sabrina Orah Mark

Hush Sessions by Kristi Maxwell

To the Bone by Sebastian Agudelo
Winner of the Saturnalia Books Poetry Prize 2008

Days of Unwilling by Cal Bedient

Letters to Poets: Conversations about Poetics, Politics, and Community
edited by Jennifer Firestone and Dana Teen Lomax

Famous Last Words by Catherine Pierce
Winner of the Saturnalia Books Poetry Prize 2007

Dummy Fire by Sarah Vap
Winner of the Saturnalia Books Poetry Prize 2006

Correspondence by Kathleen Graber
Winner of the Saturnalia Books Poetry Prize 2005

The Babies by Sabrina Orah Mark
Winner of the Saturnalia Books Poetry Prize 2004

Polytheogamy by Timothy Liu / Artwork by Greg Drasler
Artist/Poet Collaboration Series Number Five

Midnights by Jane Miller / Artwork by Beverly Pepper
Artist/Poet Collaboration Series Number Four

Stigmata Errata Etcetera by Bill Knott / Artwork by Star Black
Artist/Poet Collaboration Series Number Three

Ing Grish by John Yau / Artwork by Thomas Nozkowski
Artist/Poet Collaboration Series Number Two

Blackboards by Tomaz Salamun / Artwork by Metka Krasovec
Artist/Poet Collaboration Series Number One

Gurlesque was printed using the fonts Rosewood and Fournier.